VOLUME 17 TEX-WIN

THE PRACTICAL ENCYCLOPEDIA OF
Good Decorating
and Home Improvement

GREYSTONE PRESS

Alphabetically arranged and fully illustrated, your *Practical Encyclopedia of Good Decorating and Home Improvement* has been planned for your convenience and immediate use. In feature articles you will find a wealth of facts, ideas, suggestions, and advice that will help you solve your decorating problems. A Master/Guide at the back of each volume includes concise articles of historical interest, definitions of terms, and summaries of feature articles in the volume. Helpful cross-references appear throughout all volumes. On many pages you will find illustrations and descriptions of Project Plans and Home Plans, identified by the abbreviations PP and HP. For information on ordering these plans, write to Good Decorating Plans Editor, Greystone Press, 225 Park Avenue South, New York, N.Y. 10003.

Vary the Visual and Tactile Looks
For Greater Significance

Texture is the music of surfaces, and the notes are many and distinct. The smoothness of silk, the prickliness of burlap, the deep glow of polished wood, the cool irregularity of fieldstone: these are just a few of the great number of textural "voices" that can be orchestrated to provide rich and satisfying harmonies in decorating.

Originally, the word texture was applied only to fabrics and was variously qualified to describe effects determined by the material, size, and arrangement of interwoven threads. In time, texture came to refer to the surface quality of any object as experienced by the sense of touch; in the broadest aesthetic sense, a texture is the image of a tactile sensation formed by stimulation of the eye. An integral part of all visual perception, texture combines with the qualities of color and form to evoke the subtle feelings that characterize aesthetic response.

A wide variety of textures compensates for the limited range of colors used in an exciting light-filled living room. An opulent deep-pile rug contrasts effectively with a sleek glass-topped table, smooth plaster walls, the glossy shade of a chrome-based lamp, and glass sliding doors in aluminum tracks. The mottled fabric on the stool resembles an animal skin, while the sofa fabric suggests wide bands of interwoven ribbon. The velvety draperies and upholstery of the chairs add yet another textural note. The striking poster at the far end of the room coordinates the rectangular shapes of the table, couch, and rug with the circular forms of the lamp, chairs, and stool by arranging ovals and crescents in a strong, essentially rectangular pattern. Glimpses of concrete, brick, and natural-colored wood are visible on the terrace, where white canvas-and-wood director's chairs continue the color scheme.

A decorating tool

In decorating, texture makes an important contribution that should not be overlooked. A lively interplay of textures adds a dimension of immediacy to your basic visual elements, heightening the effects of pattern and color, and bringing a sensuous resonance to relationships among objects and materials.

When you classify materials and furnishings according to texture, you will find a wealth of interesting possibilities to work with: fabric, wood, fur, glass, brick, metal, stone, leather, cork, and plastic can all be considered for the degree of richness and contrast you desire. Basically, textures can be distinguished as rough, smooth, hard, and soft, but these categories include a broad range of individual effects.

Texture and mood

Picture a room full of smooth shiny surfaces such as glass, chrome, marble, metal, and plastic; the effect will be cold and impersonal.

On the other hand, a room saturated with soft neutral-toned elements may produce a feeling of heaviness and enclosure. Just as you can use color to create different moods, you can convey specific impressions through the skillful arrangement of textures.

The juxtaposition of contrasting materials works to intensify the character of individual elements. A shaggy light-colored rug brings out the beauty of dark highly polished floors, and a piece of gleaming silver will enhance a deep-toned walnut table.

Pattern and visual texture

Although pattern, strictly speaking, is different from texture, the two can often be manipulated to produce similar effects. Created by the arrangement of visual images, patterns stimulate varying degrees of "tactile" sensation as the eye "touches" elements that appear to stand out against an illusory depth. A blank wall will seem smooth; a geometrical pattern will give a

A 3,000-year-old slab of rosewood dominates this intriguing ▶ conversation pit. The circular shape of the wood is repeated in a variety of materials, from the pebble-encrusted concrete of the terraces to the delicate paper Japanese lantern; it is picked up in the pattern of the hand-hooked rug and in the diverse smaller objects. An acrylic bubble fills the window, reflecting minute changes in light. Bronze and stone are introduced in the statue of a woman that stands on a cylindrical granite pedestal. Lumber "boats" with worn surfaces serve as built-in tables. Richly stained walls, a fur throw rug, and a scattering of vivid pillows increase the textural interest of the setting and soften the rigid contours. Several skillfully placed plants bring a touch of life and vibrant green coloring to this precisely conceived architectural tour-de-force.

In terms of area, walls are inevitably a dominant feature in any room; an interesting surface treatment can set the tone for the rest of the decor. In a family room, the walls have been covered with bark-textured cork paneling that imparts a warm, congenial feeling to the surroundings. The cork, which comes in 12-inch squares, can be glued to the wall with contact cement. The cork treatment is enhanced by the light-colored calligraphic Chinese painting, and by the rich orange tones of the paisley print upholstery. Cheerful yellow chrysanthemums subtly reinforce the Oriental theme and, with the yellow pillow and brass accessories on the tile-topped table, add sparkle to the earthen tones and textures of sofas and walls.

wall the appearance of a continuous relief; and an irregular pattern composed of slashes of color will "roughen" the surface considerably. You can create dramatic textural interest by taking advantage of such optical illusions.

How to begin

In planning your distribution of textures, review your house or apartment room by room and analyze the many available means of implementing the effects that you desire. Be quite precise about your intentions because an over-all effect, such as the warmth or formality of a living room or the cozy familiarity of a bedroom, is always the result of a careful evaluation of detail, and texture will be important in establishing mood and subtlety of character. After the atmosphere of each room is defined in a clear-cut way, you will need a working knowledge of materials and their uses in order to execute your plans effectively. Most rooms are certain to include both wood and fabric; the challenge lies in the fact that for the rooms you are planning you have at your disposal hundreds

Neutral colors and transparent materials that reflect and transmit light can make a small space seem larger. The glass-topped chrome table sparkles under an acrylic chandelier whose vertical lines are repeated in the shimmering wall of corrugated aluminum. Silver-and-beige-patterned wallpaper adds to the glow and dazzle of the dining nook. A shaggy red-orange rug, a couple of throw pillows, a vaseful of dark dried leaves, and a precise black-and-white painting are focal points of contrasting textures that relieve the otherwise almost too sleek room.

of fabrics and scores of available woods, each with its own distinctive texture and color.

The versatility of fabric

Although fabric is most often used for upholstery, window coverings, lampshades, pillows, and cushions, it can also serve to cover walls, doors, and ceilings. In addition to the basic natural fibers—cotton, linen, silk, and wool—you can choose from a wide range of synthetics such as rayon, nylon, acetates, and polyesters.

Textural differences will depend, in part, on how the fabric is processed. It may be bonded; fused, as in the case of felt; woven; knitted; twisted, as in lace-making; or extruded, as in the fabrication of sheet plastic.

Fabrics are available in different weights for different purposes. In covering a window, for instance, you can select among textures that range from gauzelike voiles and organdies—when light is wanted but the preservation of privacy is not a consideration—to opaque, unevenly textured antique satins and homespuns. Fabrics commonly used for upholstery include patterned brocades, matelassés, and damasks; nappy corduroys; multicolored pebbly tweeds; and plush velvets and velveteens.

In choosing fabrics, be bold and inventive. The imaginative use of fabric is one of the easiest ways of creating textural interest in a room, and when you wish to modify a decorating scheme, fabric changes are easily made. If you are unable to find the right fabric for your scheme, you can try making your own through tie-dyeing, block printing, or needlework. Introduce touches of bold texture and brilliant color into a conventional room by covering pillows, cushions, or even lampshades with the wildest material you can find.

The beauty of wood

Despite the versatility of synthetic materials, wood continues to be one of the most visible structural elements in a house. It may be used in floors, walls, or ceilings; in furniture; or for

A small dining area acquires richness and apparent spaciousness through the use of textural contrasts that deepen a color scheme limited to black and a few earth tones. Adding visual depth and providing a textural foil for the rough-sawn cedar wall paneling, a tall mirror panel to the left of the dining ensemble reflects black window shutters and a shelf-wall displaying luminous pottery and glassware. A framed mirror above the table shows the kitchen area, and its reflection holds a suggestion of distance in a patch of blue sky. A contemporary dining room set contributes bold accents of wood and wrought iron, while the suede covering on the chairs provides a subtle contrast to the warm tones and semi-rough surfaces of the rug and ceiling.

accessories. Patterns and textures depend on the kind of wood and on how it has been cut and finished. Some woods, such as Douglas fir, are coarse-grained. Others—mahogany, walnut, birch, and maple are familiar examples—are close-grained and consequently much prized in cabinetmaking. The grain may be more or less prominent depending on whether a board was cut at right angles or parallel to the grain, or was stripped in a thin sheet from a rotating log and used as a veneer.

Stain, varnish, shellac, linseed oil, wax, lacquer, or paint can further alter the natural textures as they impart sheen and color to the wood.

The effect of wood

If you want to make a room look cozy and luxurious, use lots of stained or natural-colored wood. Nothing is more beautiful than a highly polished parquet floor or old wide floorboards darkly colored with age. Wood paneling on the walls can make a large room seem intimate or impart interest to a room of moderate size. Used structurally to create built-in bookshelves or cabinets, wood will provide a sense of substantiality and completeness, and it will contrast effectively with plainer surfaces elsewhere.

If you have an appropriate opportunity, consider wood for a ceiling. Exposed beams seem strong and protective. They bring into a room a suggestion of the past as they contrast evocatively with a white plaster ceiling, or complement a handsome wooden roof by creating their own rhythmic pattern. Depending on whether beams run parallel or at right angles to the main axis of a room, they can accentuate its length or emphasize its width. Placed on a sloping ceiling, they will draw attention to the height of the room.

Metal: a bright spot in any room

Metal, the workhorse of the modern house, can also be featured as a central ornament. Most houses utilize four tons of inconspicuous metal in the mundane and durable forms of nails and screws, insulation, structural supports, pipes, electric wiring, furnaces, kitchen appliances, cooking utensils, radiators, and hardware. More and more, however, it is being used for furniture and wall coverings as well as for the more traditional decorative items.

Metal is a very ancient material, but it is only since the Industrial Revolution of the early nineteenth century that metal products could be mass produced and begin to find their way into most people's homes. The new industrial processes made the manufacture of even the most intricate shapes inexpensive, and designers of the Victorian period went wild with elaborate and fanciful ornamentation.

Today, in line with the idea that form should follow function, metal is used in ways that emphasize its smooth surfaces and clean lines. Chromium, called chrome for short, is the metal favored by many furniture designers. Since it is shiny and hard, it is often combined with glass or contrasted with leather.

Because of the association of certain metals with specific historical eras, you will find, if you are creating a period room, that some metals blend better than others. Silver, copper, pewter, and brass are appropriate with eighteenth-century furnishings. Brass frequently has an Oriental character that also goes well with contemporary furniture. Wrought iron, as has been mentioned, was a nineteenth-century development, and much of it is available in typical patterns of that period, while chrome, aluminum, and stainless steel are inescapably modern.

These are not meant as hard-and-fast rules, but simply as guidelines that will suggest where to start if you are selecting metal accents for a room of unified style.

Other materials

In decorating your house, you will find that you now have a wider range of materials to choose from than ever before. Use them imaginatively and lavishly! Many of these new materials, particularly the various forms of plastic, are quite practical in addition to being beautiful, unusual, and, in many cases, inexpensive.

However, if you do go wild with textures, keep in mind that you have to maintain some unity in a room. The three design elements available to the decorator are texture, form, and color. If you concentrate on the use of texture in a room, obviously the other elements must become secondary considerations; you must either work within a limited color scheme *or* select furnishings and accessories whose line and shape establish distinct patterns with comparatively subtle visual distinctions. Thus you can establish a framework within which successful concentration on texture is possible.

Dramatic richness is the keynote of a small grouping centered around a wall-hung writing table that glows with metallic accents. The vivid play of light and color is effectively varied by the different surfaces: the vibrant red lacquer and chrome of the chairs, the deep coffee-brown walls, and the leather of screen and chair. An earth-toned shag rug and a painting with touches of impasto bring textural counterpoint to a shimmering atmosphere.

TILING

The Full How-To of Applying All Types of Tiles

In recent years, tiling walls and floors has become a popular do-it-yourself activity—small wonder since the material comes in convenient sizes that are much more manageable than sheet goods and installation is easily done with adhesive. Even the do-it-yourselfer unblessed with more than the usual complement of thumbs can do a good job.

While simple, it is not just a matter of laying the material in place. First, there are differences between tile types that make one more suitable than another in a given area. Also, the surface—floor or wall—that the tile is to cover must be carefully considered.

■ Ceramic tile: this type has long been the standard material for bathroom walls and floors, primarily because it stands up to water so well. Since it is very easy to maintain and can take much abuse, it has also found its way into entry halls, kitchens (especially the area above the sink), and family rooms. And, simply because it is so good-looking, some people have installed it in living and dining rooms, even though its special toughness is not really required.

For bathrooms, glazed wall tile and ceramic mosaic tile have proved most popular. In the past, the former was used strictly for walls, the latter for floors; but today, as trends shift toward experimentation, they are interchangeable.

■ Glazed wall tile: this type is available in over 1,000 shades and color combinations and innumerable designs and sizes. For walls, the most popular are the $4\frac{1}{4}$x$4\frac{1}{4}$-inch, $4\frac{1}{4}$x6-inch, and 6x6-inch sizes. When buying, get all the tiles for the job from one manufacturer. Tile sizes, nominally the same, can vary up to $\frac{1}{4}$ inch from brand to brand.

Ceramic mosaic tile is a little thinner than glazed tile, and comes in smaller (1x1-inch and 1x2-inch) pieces. These are mounted on a backing in 1x1- and 1x2-foot sheets, which speeds the job considerably. Individual tiles in the sheet may be square, hexagonal, octagonal, or other shapes. The glaze also varies. They can be shiny, matte-glazed, or extra-duty glazed for floors. Generally, the highly glazed tiles are easiest to keep clean, while their unglazed counterparts withstand more abuse.

In the past, installation of ceramic tile involved setting it in a mortar bed, over a surface covered with building paper and then metal lath. The job required considerable skill, and all but the most skilled do-it-yourselfers left the job to the professional.

Adhesive installation is simple. The adhesive is applied with a special notched spreader, either borrowed or rented from the tile dealer, and the tiles of whatever kind laid directly on it. You can use this method on any kind of wall, as long as it does not have any irregularities or depressions that will throw the tiles out of line. If this is the case, you can purchase special fillers from your dealer to level the surface first.

On walls that are in constant contact with water, such as in a shower enclosure or around the tub, it is best to rip out the old wall material, say plasterboard, and replace it with an

Tiles that have long been associated with use in one room have found their way into other areas. Stainless steel wall tiles add an unusual luminous touch to a living room. Metal tile is usually installed with adhesive, but some have adhesive tabs on the back.

underlayment of either ½-inch exterior C-C plugged plywood or ½-inch vinyl-surfaced wallboard.

Wood floors to be tiled would be standard double-wood floors, that is, ¾-inch boards or ¾- to ⅝-inch plywood on the joists plus an overlay of ⅜-inch exterior plugged plywood.

The best adhesive to use when tiling is a matter to discuss with your dealer. Different kinds are used depending on the material to which you are adhering the tile.

■ Plastic wall tile: this is much lower in cost than ceramic tile. It is available in a great variety of bright colors and has proved popular for bathrooms. Application of the plastic tiles—with a standard size of about 4½x4½ inches—is done with adhesive.

■ Metal wall tile: this is also installed with adhesive. It can be either steel or aluminum with a baked enamel finish or ceramic coat, or just plain copper or stainless steel. This type is most frequently used in the kitchen. The standard size is 4½x4½ inches and some types can be used where moisture is a problem.

■ Resilient tile: installation of this type is even simpler than for ceramic tile. It is available in 9-inch and 12-inch squares in a virtually endless number of styles and colors, with surfaces that are textured, smooth, glossy, and non-glossy. You can get tiles that simulate other materials, including brick and marble. As a group, resilient tiles are probably the most popular flooring. See *Resilient Floor Covering,* Vol. 15, p. 2786.

Tiling a Wall with Plastic or Metal Tiles

The only special tool you will require for this job is an adhesive spreader; cut plastic tile with a coping or finishing saw, metal tile with tin snips or a hacksaw. Begin by finding the low spot in a room. Measure up *each* wall to the tile height wanted (longest measurement from the floor is the lowest point). Calculate the height by placing the bottom tile on the low wall at least an inch below the bottom line. This will allow you room for later fitting.

Mark number of rows needed, starting little below line at lowest point. Include feature strip (if it is to be used), but not cap strip, which is installed last. Pencil line up wall for vertical guide; figure rows with a tile.

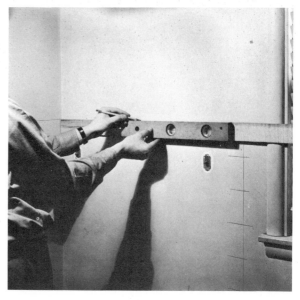

Pencil a horizontal line completely around room at tile height, starting at the perpendicular line. Use a level. Cap strip extends above the line. Scrap plywood was tacked onto the level in picture, giving a longer marking edge.

From the center of the wall, mark vertical guidelines with a tile. Start flush to the center line; mark to the corners. If *less* than half a tile width occurs at either corner, *center* the tile on the center line and mark.

Patch cracks and holes, especially around bathtub and lavatory. Make sure patches are completely dry before starting tiling. Run a straightedge over wall to find high spots, and mark them. Level them with No. 1 sandpaper.

Spread mastic with the notched spreader, and comb out in vertical lines. Poor bonding occurs when too little mastic is used (a gallon covers 40 to 50 square feet). Ridges will flatten and fill up the backs of the tiles.

Start tiling where vertical and horizontal guidelines meet. Lay two vertical rows, then two horizontal rows. Slip tile off the beveled edge of adjoining one (see picture) to get a tight joint. Press to the wall.

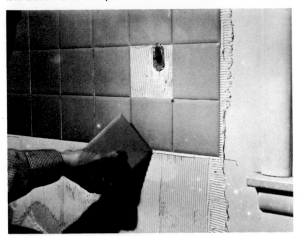

Level mastic ridges below row of tiles that have just been laid. This smooths out excess mastic and gives clean horizontal joints. Do not slip the tiles up, down, or sideways in the mastic as you apply them.

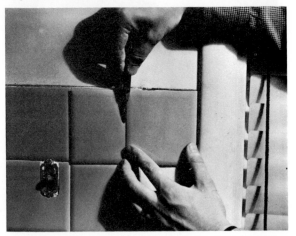

For fitting, hold tile to be fitted atop full tile it joins. Put another tile over area to be covered, so it overlaps the tile to be cut. Scribe along edge of the top tile onto the bottom one, then cut it to the line.

Outside corner (use molded corner tile) goes on first; then work toward inside one. Always put joining edges tight against each other. Tile pushed against another plows up mastic. Tiles "float" if too much mastic is used.

Clean the joints carefully with pointed stick or corner of the tile. Regular cleaner removes hard mastic; fresh smears come off with a soft cloth. When you have laid a field of tile, clean off excess mastic.

Undercut plaster around bathtub and lavatory so mastic fills the crack and assures a tight seal between tile, plaster, and tub or lavatory. Thoroughly clean crevice before you apply the mastic coat.

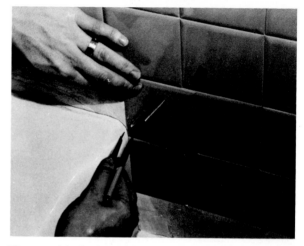

Fit around bathtub and lavatory by scribing cut with a pencil compass. Points are set to width of overlap of tile (arrow). Holding compass horizontal, let steel point follow rim of tub where it joins the wall.

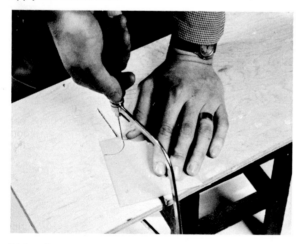

Make circular cuts with a coping saw for fitting plastic tile. Use a hacksaw or tin snips for metal. Plywood jig here has a cut that allows space for the blade. Line up saw with the slot; turn the tile for cutting.

Straight cuts on plastic tile are easy with fine-tooth saw held at flat angle with jig. Use hacksaw same way for straight metal cuts. Regular plane smoothes edges of plastic tile or does final fitting after sawing.

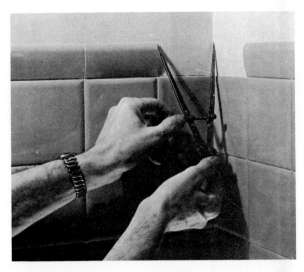

Tile around fixtures that you cannot remove from the wall by first cutting away plaster around them with a knife or chisel. To get a closer fit, bevel the edges of the tiles that will adjoin fixtures. It is best to remove the fixtures whenever you possibly can.

The cap strip completes the tiling job. Scribe for miter cut on outside and inside corners with the dividers. Measure from cap strip so that the mitered piece will adjoin corner of the wall. Transfer measurement to the piece to be mitered and then saw on the line.

Flexible Plastic Wall Tile Comes Prepasted

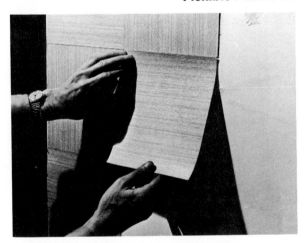

Flexible plastic tiles are prepasted and ready to apply to ceilings and walls of plaster, plywood, plasterboard, hardboard, and so on. Tiles are 8x8 inches in size. Patterns are deep-textured, in colors or in simulated wood grains.

Application to walls is easy due to flexibility. Tiles can be bent and cut to fit any area, such as in the bathroom around tub, lavatory, and flush tank. Complete installation instructions are furnished by the dealer.

Tiling a Wall with Ceramic Tiles

Materials needed for setting ceramic tiles include the tile and accessories, tile adhesive, wall primer, grout, notched adhesive spreader, glass cutter, pliers, plastic sponge, and a paintbrush. In using ceramic tiles, you can employ the same precision measuring techniques described for working with plastic and metal tiles, just preceding. Either determine the low point in the room and start measuring from there, or set the first tiles around the top rim of the bathtub. If you want to start with tiles around the edge of the tub, you may save yourself some trimming; the only row that will have to be cut will be tiles next to the floor. As in any tiling job, a smooth and level wall is necessary.

(continued)

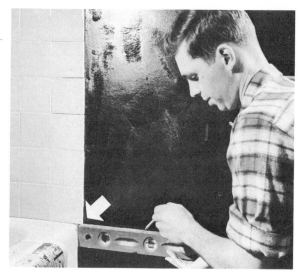

Start tiling around bathtub after you have leveled the walls, sanded down any rough spots, and primed walls with a sealer. Be especially careful to keep the first row of tiles level. To keep adhesive from drying before the tiles are set in place, spread it over a small area. Keep it fairly thick—about the amount that flows from the applicator. Use twisting motion to press tiles in place.

To tile away from the bathtub, mark a straight line out with a level (as shown) and tile from that line down to the floor. This method keeps all tiles that have to be cut next to the floor line. Pliers or nippers will cut tiles to fit around the rim of the tub (arrow). Protect finish of the bathtub and other bathroom fixtures with newspapers or dropcloths; this will save a lot of cleaning up.

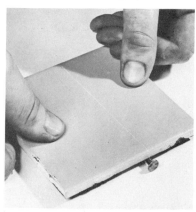

Scribe for fitting by overlapping tile to be fitted over edge of next one. Mark cutoff point on back of tile; transfer to face of another. Then cut on the line.

To cut tiles, score the face with a glass cutter. Place tile over sixteenpenny or twentypenny nail so nail is in line with cutoff, and press down on the edges.

Tile around pipes and other permanent fixtures in this manner: slice tile in half and nibble out a semicircle in center of the pieces with pliers or nippers.

Soap dish is installed after the tiles. Remove two tiles, apply adhesive to wall and back of fixture and press into position. Cut and fit tiles around edges.

Cap strip and corner tiles go on after field tiles are at the height you want. Avoid smearing adhesive above cap strip. If you do, wipe it off immediately.

Grout the joints after the adhesive sets a day or so. Wet joints first with water (about 4 gallons for a bathroom) to keep tiles from drawing water from grout.

Installing Floor Tiles on Walls

Floor tiles are small ceramic tiles that come in prespaced groups called "squares." They are applied as a unit to the wall, and then a paper facing that holds the squares in place is removed, leaving the face of the tiles exposed.

Start just as with other tiles. Find the low spot around the bathtub, establish horizontal and vertical guidelines, and spread adhesive with a notched spreader. Apply only a small amount of adhesive at a time.

Press paper-faced tile into adhesive. Tap each square *lightly* in place with rubber hammer. Chalk line (arrow) spaces joints between the squares.

Before mastic sets, match joint lines between high and low points in room. Cut paper facing; jockey rows of tiles up or down to compensate.

Remove individual tiles around fixtures; collar flanges may cover tile edges so you will not have to cut them. Fixtures are set in the wall with adhesive.

To continue pattern next to the moldings, interchange tiles—narrow for wide and vice versa—and stick in place with mastic. For narrow spaces, cut the tiles.

Trowel grout into the joints, let set a few minutes, and wipe off the excess. Then wipe tiles dry with a soft cloth. Let job set a few days before using.

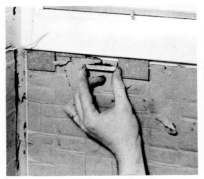

TRIMMINGS

Appreciate the Value of Adding That Little Extra Something

Trimmings are a little like lipstick. A girl can be pretty without it—but it makes a delightful difference. A room can be decorated carefully and tastefully, and yet lack a certain fillip—a fillip that trimmings can supply.

Of course, like lipstick, trimmings can be overdone. Apply them only as a finishing touch; you do not want a heavy layer of extras to mask your basic room scheme. Trimmings should add, not overwhelm. To accomplish this, choose trimmings that blend with the decor in color, mood, and style, and keep their distribution proportionate to their function.

The trim is the thing

In order to exploit the decorative power of trimmings, you must familiarize yourself with the many types and kinds available. Visit the decorating or fabric department of a department store, or explore a decorating shop, and you will find a world of exciting trims—braids, fringe, iron-on tapes, ribbons, rickrack, and tassels. Just as fashion fabrics have become more and more sophisticated and varied in recent years, so have decorating accessories, and you should avail yourself of the opportunity to handle and compare the various kinds of trimmings; they can often provide the inspiration for a room scheme.

Another way to become familiar with trimmings is to analyze magazine photographs of rooms you admire to see how trimming has

contributed to the overall effect. Often, the trim is almost, but not quite, unnoticeable—a simple band of printed tape outlining a valance, or a row of ball fringe half concealed under a bedspread's canopy skirt. When you picture the same room without that final touch, it is apparent that trimming has made the difference.

Architectural uses

Trimmings are customarily used for exclusively decorative purposes, but they can also lend themselves to the creation of architectural ef-

You can use different types and styles of trimming in one ▶ room and still achieve a harmonious effect if you exercise care in selecting them. Here, a Mediterranean theme dictated the choice. With four different kinds of trimming— ball fringe, loop fringe, braid, and ribbon tassels—the room presents a unified atmosphere because all of the trimmings share the exuberance and relaxed design typical of decor that expresses a Spanish mood. The ball fringe echoes the beads of the chandelier; this detail does much to make the trimmings seem at home in the setting. The ball fringe could have been repeated on the round tablecloth, but the use of the loop fringe increases the intricacy of the effect. Note the braid on the chairs—it combines qualities of both the loop and the ball fringe.

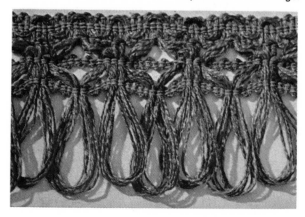

The colorful loop fringe used on the round tablecloth shown in the sketch is reproduced here about half its actual size; the same scale is used in the other details of individual trims appearing in this article.

An unusual place for fringe—a stairway carpet. Wool-knot rug fringe, conventionally used on area rugs, adds visual interest to a traditional stairway. This treatment would be especially effective if combined with a nearby area rug trimmed with the same fringe.

An area rug looks as though it was custom-made for the setting. Actually, it is a standard-size rug that was moved from an apartment to a new home. The rug was measured, cut in a different shape to fit the new dining area, and then trimmed with a wool braid that gave it renewed life and color. This pattern was chosen because it fits the contemporary mood of the house; its colors go beautifully with the rug color, and the design has enough boldness to make an effective decorating point.

A canopy adds elegance to outdoor meals on the patio. The awning fabric is waterproof, as are the delightful tassels that add the finishing touch to each of the strips forming the canopy. The strips are channeled so that the horizontal rod can pass through them, securing them in place. Additional strips of awning material are used to decorate the table.

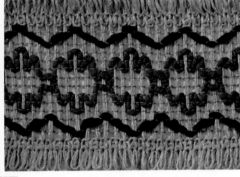

You can use trimming as a "construction material," as in this open-plan contemporary house. Drapery rods at floor and ceiling hold strips of burlap braid, hemmed and slipped over the rods. The panel of strips creates the illusion of a dividing wall, although the open design prevents a closed-in effect. The same idea could be applied to a window. Here, the dividing "wall" separates the living room from the entrance hall without sacrificing the spaciousness of the open plan. The burlap braid has an interesting texture, and the strands of colored yarn woven into the design supply tonal effect.

fects. Try the comparatively simple technique of using trimming to simulate molding on a fabric wall, or consider trim for more complex functions—as dividers, valances, or "frames" for windows or doors. You can lower a ceiling by creating a tentlike canopy around the ceiling, using fabric and tasseled fringe for trim. Construct a pretend canopy for a bed by attaching a hanging fringe to an outline drawn on the ceiling.

Decorative versatility

Trimmings have a thousand decorative uses. They can transform a closet from a simple storage box into a decorative bonus. You can use trimmings to turn ready-mades into custom-made furnishings; a simple slipcover looks very different when the back cushion and bottom flounce are decorated with braid or ribbon trim. Curtains and bedspreads, bought inexpensively, can be decorated with a ribbon trim that covers seams and adds a luxury touch.

You can frame a window with a plywood frame covered in fabric and then dress it up with a wide braid trim. The same kind of wide braid can be used in a bedroom. Position a rectangle of felt as a vertical "headboard" for a bed that is covered with a matching felt bedspread. Then apply wide braid vertically down the center of the panel and the bedspread.

In a dining room, you can use wide wallpaper borders as "moldings"; then apply the same border to a window valance. In a white dining room, a border of blue and pink roses

could be used in this way. The curtains might be blue, with ball fringe in blue, pink, and white as trim. Chairs slipcovered in a small rose pattern would complete the scheme.

Ball fringe is a versatile trim because it comes in so many sizes and colors. The combination of ball fringe and unbleached muslin makes a

An imaginative idea—using lacy iron gates as twin-bed headboards—was immeasurably enhanced by the use of a trimming. Complementing the ironwork, crisp charcoal-and-white eyelet embroidery in a medallion design borders the draperies and bedspreads. The floral upholstery fabric, with its repetition of charcoal and white, provides the counterpoint needed to strengthen the total effect. The accent color, red, subtly emphasizes the Spanish feeling introduced by the scrollwork and embroidery. Almost every element in this room is important to the overall effect, but it is the trimming that contributes the stamp of individuality to the room.

happy choice for "country" curtains. Large-scale crochet trim has the same casual look.

Creative trimming

Macrame, the ancient art of creative knot-tying, has recently recovered the popularity it enjoyed in Victorian times. This type of trim blends very well with Victorian decor and looks wonderful dripping from valances or decorating lampshades. Macrame, like crocheting, affords a creative expression as well as a decorative solution. See *Macrame,* Vol. 12, p. 2166.

One reason trimmings are so much fun to work with is that they may be combined or

A teen-ager will delight in this sophisticated version of the traditional girl's room with canopy bed and floral pattern. The print brings a fresh look to the floral pattern, and the design of the canopy is as modern as tomorrow. The canopy framework could be copied using standard lumber. The campaign-chest furniture units are available in an unpainted version that you can finish yourself. To make the fabric canopy panel, you simply hem a length of fabric cut to the right measure and attach the large-scale swags of ball-fringe trim. If you attach the fringe with large basting stitches, it can be removed to make laundering easier. The tablecover is almost as easy to make. Use a pencil attached to a string as a compass and mark a circumference on the fabric; hem and attach the fringe. Unless fabric is unusually wide, it will be necessary to seam two or more widths together; be sure to match the fabric pattern so that it appears seamless. Curtains and valance might repeat the scheme, or you can use a solid color and trim it with the fringe.

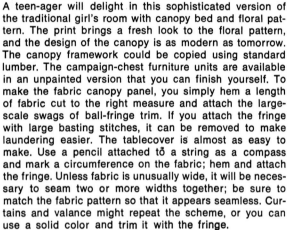

adapted to so many different uses. Even so simple a thing as plastic tape—in bright colors —can be used to trim the edge of a valance or to apply a design on a plain plywood door. Another creative element is the manner in which you use the material.

Rickrack, for instance, can be a stereotyped and rather naïve decorative trim if it is used in the traditional single-line-around-the-edge way. However, when it is sewn in multiple rows with no spaces intervening, it takes on a more sophisticated look. Rickrack and flat braid can be combined to make borders that look almost Greek in their classic simplicity; and several different kinds of flat braid can be used together to form Indian- or Peruvian-type designs.

A ribbon press-on trim can transform an inexpensive shower curtain. Just apply several rows to the bottom edge of the curtains.

Ruffles can be used as trimming. A traditional white organdy bedspread can be freshened by adding a ruffle of bright plaid gingham under the bottom organdy ruffle; then hang a short ruffle from the top edges of the spread.

White fishnet can be used as a drapery swag panel, held in place with loops of white roping to give a nautical look to a family room. The same roping could outline the edges of blue sofa cushions.

With so many wonderful trimmings to choose from, how do you select just the right touch for the room you are planning?

Choosing the right trim

The key word is *appropriate*. When you come to choose the trimming, you know whether the room is formal or informal; you have settled on the color scheme, the mood, the period or style;

and you know whether the scale is large and flamboyant or small and trim. All of these factors must weigh in the balance. The texture of the fabric makes a difference: burlap and felt are a good combination; eyelet embroidery looks wonderful on organdy, as does narrow velvet ribbon. Silk draperies require an elegant trim; simple gingham curtains look best treated simply, with cotton ball fringe, narrow binding, or rickrack.

The world of fashion can be a source of inspiration when you are searching for appropriate trimmings. For instance, to tie back draperies in a Spanish-mood room, you might use the kind of decorative braid frogs that trim the jackets of a matador. A museum of primitive crafts or books on fashion design will give you suggestions concerning harmonious combinations. The fashion classic of a monochrome jacket with a print lining and a band of print trim can be adapted to make curtains. Line the curtains with a floral print, and pin them back with a flower-shaped tack so the lining shows.

On the outside of the hem, add a band of the flower print, then complete the decorating ensemble by slipcovering a chair or sofa with the printed fabric.

Any fabric panel can become a swag with standard drapery loops mounted at the top corners of the window. A border of fringe or ball trim will give the drapery a finished look. You can use the swag alone, or pair it with long tailored curtains with a matching trim at the bottom hems.

Pairing a trimming used at the windows with a trim on a bedspread, an upholstered piece, or another piece of furniture helps to coordinate the trimming with the room. In front of a pair of windows, for instance, you can place a Parsons table. Frame the windows in a flat border of plywood, covered with fabric and trimmed with flat braid. Add café curtains of the same fabric. Paint the Parsons table to match the fabric, and then paste the flat braid around the table border. The result is a desk-study corner that looks like a single unit.

Panels of fabric were used in this room to create an alcove. The panels were hung from the ceiling molding to the dado. A trimming of braid was used to outline the panels, making them clearly defined areas of color. Architecturally, the braid performs the function of a molding. The placement of the panels, with one of them "turning the corner," sets off the sofa and end table. Because the room's walls were dark, light panels were used to stress the separation.

An ordinary pair of windows has been transformed in this charming bedroom. Separated by a strip of wall, they looked old-fashioned and awkward. Now they have been turned into a unit by the use of a unifying board valance and a vertical strip of mirror between the two windows. Once architectural unity was achieved, decorative unity was provided by the canny combination of window shades and curtains trimmed with the same lovely braid.

A length of heavy wool fabric can become an afghan if it is bordered with deep fringe in a heavy weight that matches the heavy texture of the wool.

Denim, an inexpensive fabric for a child's room, can be high style if you iron on "patches" of decorative trim in bright glowing colors, just as you might iron patches onto a pair of denim blue jeans. You can cut out fanciful shapes, or simply use rectangles, circles, and squares of color.

Bias tape can also be used as trimming, wherever you might use flat braid. For example, use bias tape for a striped effect on solid color curtains, or subdivide panels of fabric with it.

Coordinating the trim

Printed window shades are fun and can substitute for window curtains. But they will look more finished if they are supplemented with a border trim, either on the window frame or on a valance made from plywood.

The same type of relationship works well if the trimming is used in a small area such as a dining alcove. In a small white alcove, scalloped valances of blue with white coin dots could be added above small windows hung with sheer white café curtains. Cut several sets of place mats from a length of the same fabric and match them with solid blue napkins. If curtains have tasseled pull-back ties, put tassels on a pillow that matches the color of the draperies and toss it on a nearby sofa.

Using appliqués is another way to coordinate trimming with a room scheme. You can use a cutout flower of floral chintz as a trimming on solid-color curtains. In a kitchen, you can appliqué fruit or vegetable cutouts that match a motif in the kitchen wallpaper.

Ball fringe looks pert around the circular seat of an ice-cream parlor chair—either attach it directly or sew it to the cushions. The same trim might look well on a cushion for a piano stool; in a playroom, you might attach the trim around the top of an upright piano.

Trim, large and small

You can use decorative trimmings on small accessories as well as with major pieces. Your loose-leaf recipe book will look fresh and attractive if it is covered in kitchen-curtain material and trimmed with rickrack or tape.

A small mirror on a beruffled dressing table can be outlined with a similar ruffle. A mirror over a small shelf presents the choice of trimming the edge of the shelf with a loop edging also used on the mirror.

Simple window shades and matching fabrics on a table and chair combine to produce a cheerful summery look in this living room. The trim is velvety nylon ribbon; on the shades, pressure-sensitive tape was used, and heat-sensitive tape was ironed onto the fabric. When you apply the tape, pencil guidelines on the shades so that you can apply the tape in alignment on both shades. You can baste the tape on the fabric before ironing it. Using such easy-to-apply tape means that you can work with ready-made slipcovers and plain window shades and still create a custom-made look.

Sheets trimmed with ruffles make inexpensive curtains, and you can use an extra sheet to make twin swag valances, looping them up with lengths of ruffles sewn together in a wide strip.

Effect and restraint

One word of caution, however. As you try more and more uses for trimming, and become familiar with the wide range of trimmings available, you will find that inspiration multiplies faster than opportunities for using it. Do not overdo. Always experiment with the trimming, holding it in place and checking it in the room itself before attaching it permanently. See trimmings in relation to your plan as a whole—a small part in quantity, but a vital contribution to the spirit of any decorating scheme.

TROMPE L'OEIL

Create Your Own Stage And Be an Illusionist

"Trompe l'oeil," literally translated from the French, means to deceive the eye. The illusionistic painting technique can be traced back to the ancient Greeks and was most notably revived during the Italian Renaissance.

Murals, frescoes, paintings, or wall decorations that trick the onlooker into thinking a landscape or architectural detail is real instead of an obvious representation fall into this category. Often the device is employed merely to amuse, although it can also be used effectively to open up a small enclosed room.

If you decide to use a trompe l'oeil effect in your home decoration scheme, you will be in august company. In fifteenth-century Italy, the Gonzaga family of Mantua, wanting to decorate the marriage chamber in their castle, called on the renowned Paduan painter Andrea Mantegna. Mantegna, interested in perspective and spatial illusion, created a still-extant example of trompe l'oeil in the Camera degli Sposi. By interweaving actual architectural details with painted ones, he created the illusion that the low vault of the ceiling was actually an

The wallpaper in this small dining room reproduces a spacious Victorian summerhouse. Palm trees, trellises, and a receding arch "supported" on thin columns suggest an airy, sun-dappled arbor. Carrying the illusion into reality, a whimsical birdcage, plants, and the flower-bedecked candlestick on the sideboard reinforce the image. A classic example of trompe l'oeil, the room demonstrates how you can establish a mood through the clever manipulation of painted perspectives.

A hand-painted mural provides ▶ an interesting solution to the problem of how to enliven a dead-end corner. A fantasy of country palace, water, arches, and a willow tree, it is framed by an archway of old brick. The warm tones of the brick and the coral-colored table and counter are picked up in the painting, which appears to be an extension of the room itself.

◄ The transformation of a sturdy old-fashioned armoire into a whimsical storage cabinet demonstrates that fun and profit can be derived from trompe l'oeil. The fun arises from the novelty of finding a larger-than-life contrary Mary watering her garden on the outside of a serious piece of furniture. The profit stems from the modest cost of the finished product: less than $60 for the armoire, wallpaper, pasting kit, spray plastic, water putty, and white paint.

The armoire was discovered in a thrift shop. The first step in its rehabilitation was to remove some superfluous trim and to fill in the cracks and grooves with putty. After sanding the putty and washing the whole piece with liquid sander, the entire cabinet was covered with several coats of white paint. Then the wallpaper was pasted on.

"Mary, Mary" is one of a line of wallpaper murals. The black line drawing on a white background transforms the solemn old armoire into a gay and lively piece of contemporary furniture. To apply the paper, first heavily coat the back with paste, let it soak in, and then carefully wrap the paper around the furniture. Do not bother about trying to work around the molding, doors, and hinges. After the major pasting down is finished, make slits in the paper with a sharp knife to allow the fixtures through. As you work, remove bubbles and wrinkles with a wallpaper-smoothing brush.

This particular wallpaper was designed in sheets with an overlapping pattern that would have created an unattractive ridge when used for this purpose. So the repetitious parts of the design were trimmed off before aligning the panels. Finally, after allowing the paste to dry for several days, the chest was sprayed with a clear lacquer.

oculus, a circular opening on the sky surrounded by a painted marble balustrade. Women and children appear to peep down over the edges, and chubby winged cupids perch on the rail.

If hiring a painter gifted in this technique is impractical, you can still achieve trompe l'oeil effects with wallpaper. Look for a murallike paper that represents a landscape. Your decorating task then is to combine the wallpaper skillfully with an architectural framework to create or reinforce an illusion.

If you have big picture windows and a spectacular view, you might want to try painting window shades to match the scene outside. This lovely modern house in Rockland County, New York, faces the Hudson River and High Tor Mountain. When the shades are up, foliage, water, mountains, and sky are visible, although the painted view shown here is almost as spectacular and prevents the large expanse of windows from becoming gaping black holes at night. Window shade painting is a form of trompe l'oeil that originated in the eighteenth century. A number of well-known artists have attempted the technique, including the great French impressionist, Auguste Renoir.

UPHOLSTERING

The ABC's of What to Use And How to Go About It

Today, the presence of comfortably upholstered sofas and chairs is almost always taken for granted when decorating schemes are planned for houses and apartments. And yet, upholstered furniture as we know it is a comparatively recent development in furniture design.

The term upholstery refers to the materials and techniques used in the covering and stuffing of furniture. In England, upholstered furniture was in use during the Elizabethan period, but it was not until the latter part of the seventeenth century that luxurious upholstery became a prominent feature of decorating style. The early upholstered pieces were generally covered with needlework on canvas; during the eighteenth century, when the art reached sophisticated heights, upholstery textiles included cut silk velvets, brocades, damasks, satins, tapestries, and chintzes and other printed cottons and linens. Towards the end of this period the lighter fabrics were preferred, and springs began to be used in the stuffing. The now-familiar overstuffed chair was first produced in mid-nineteenth-century France, and its shape was probably derived from the Turkish divan.

Know the inside story

Among the most important purchases that you will make are the pieces of upholstered furniture that are essential components of a comfortable and attractively designed home. Although it may not have occurred to you at the time, one of the first purchases you made can be considered upholstered furniture—a mattress and box spring.

Whether you are contemplating the purchase of a mattress, a chaise for the bedroom, or an upholstered rocker for a spot near the fireplace, the act of buying upholstered furniture is not nearly as much a matter of guesswork as it once was. Many states now require that all new items of upholstered furniture, whether ready-made or covered-to-order (including mattresses, box springs, pillows, and decorative cushions), carry labels that are well attached and that clearly list the stuffing contents. A new easy chair for your living room, therefore, might be labeled: ALL NEW MATERIAL CONSISTING OF, BODY: curled horsehair, 50%, blended cotton felt, 45%, latex rubber foam, 5%; CUSHIONS (2): goose down, 50%, goose feathers, 50%.

Such a label does more than give the consumer a list of upholstery contents that cannot be seen. It also provides important information that can be used in comparing pieces of furniture that appear to be similar in all respects except for the price. Differences in inside contents and construction may make the expected durability of one chair considerably greater than that of another with a smaller price tag. Such a difference should be given careful evaluation.

Vibrant dark carpeting, rustic paneling, and a beamed ceiling create a mellow background for the carefully chosen fabrics in this combination living room and dining room. Repetition of the black-and-white floral fabric in the draperies, sofa, and chair seats establishes a comfortable sense of unity throughout. Word of caution: all patterns do not thrive in such profusion; choose a design that you can live with. Here the yellow accents, including the mass of yellow used on the sofa, help to balance and mute the print. To change the mood of the room, which is rather autumnal, without redecorating, just change the accent from yellow to a bright red or cool green.

The walls and floor of this sunny room serve as a warm background for a handsome furniture arrangement. Two identical easy chairs, covered in the same fabric, are joined together in a visual unit by the complementary upholstery of the sofa. The chairs, although standing away from the wall, are visually held in place by tailored and kick-pleated skirts that reach the floor. An area rug of the same lush green holds the lovely setting together.

Upholstery construction

Whether you are planning to buy new upholstered furniture, or contemplating a do-it-yourself project on an old family standby, a measure of basic technical information will be useful to you. The single most important part of any upholstered piece is the frame, since it both carries the weight and determines the shape. For the frame, the most suitable woods are those least likely to split with the repeated use of upholstery tacks. Kiln-dried poplar, birch, maple, and gum are practical choices.

The frame should be securely joined for strength and support. Spiral-grooved dowels make stronger and more firmly held joints than smooth dowels; tenons and screws are both excellent for this purpose. A solidly constructed joint can also be made using high-quality glue. Nailing is the least desirable method of joining a frame. However the frame is built, the seat should be reinforced by inserting triangular blocks of wood at the inside corners. In furniture made of spring construction, the use of wood blocks at corners provides additional resistance to the tension of the springs.

Padding and stuffing

Basically, upholstered furniture falls into two categories, padded and overstuffed. In the construction of padded furniture, a layer of stuffing such as cotton felt or foam rubber is placed over a panel of wood, then covered with the final upholstery material. Overstuffed furniture contains webbing tacked to an open framework and covered with the stuffing—springs, foam, or perhaps curled hair. A layer of muslin is added and covered with the final upholstery fabric.

The webbing, generally made of jute, is attached to the frame to provide support for the springs and other stuffing materials. Jute is used for this purpose because it has little elasticity, and when properly stretched and nailed will keep its shape for a long time. The size of the frame opening and the weight to be supported determine the quantity of webbing to be used. As a rule of thumb, seats require more webbing than backs. In seats containing springs, you need at least one horizontal and one vertical row of interlaced webbing for every row of springs.

Once the webbing has been interlaced, stretched, and tacked securely to the underside of the seat rails, the springs are set into place. Upholstery springs are used to build up the foundations for the seats of overstuffed furniture. They are made of 9- to 11-gauge wire and are available in heights ranging from 4 to 14 inches; the most frequently used springs are 9 inches high. Once in place, the springs are compressed to fit the design and shape of the seat. The springs used in the backs of upholstered pieces are made of 12- to 15-gauge wire. They are called pillow springs and come in heights of 4, 6, and 8 inches. When they are placed on top of the webbing, the springs should be

as close to each other as possible without touching. They should also be arranged in straight lines to facilitate tying them down. The springs are then stitched tightly to the webbing.

When the upholstery is supported by wood slats instead of webbing, the procedure is somewhat different. It is best for the slats to be covered first with a layer of burlap or other material to prevent rattling. Staple the springs to the slats, placing one staple over each side of the bottom coil.

Tying the springs

Tying down the springs is the crucial step in the making or remaking of upholstered furniture. The condition of the springs determines the life of the furniture, and the life of the springs depends largely on the manner in which they are tied. Stretch manila or hemp twine straight across the rows of springs in both directions, and then run twine diagonally in both directions; knot each piece of twine to each top coil in two places, making eight knots for each spring. This serves to brace them against tension from all sides. The softness or hardness of an upholstered seat will be determined by the number of springs, by how loosely or tightly the springs are coiled, and by how much they are compressed when tied into position.

A covering of burlap or canvas is placed over the tied springs, followed by a layer of filling material. Whatever material is used for this layer of padding—cotton felt, kapok, Spanish moss, curled horsehair, rubberized hair, or foam rubber—it must be evenly spread to prevent lumps or wrinkles from appearing. Unbleached muslin is then stretched over the filling material and tacked securely to the seat rails. There are two reasons for using a muslin covering at this point—it keeps the padding in place and protects the final covering from strain.

Foam rubber

It should be noted that many lines of comfortable and well-designed upholstered furniture

The choice of upholstery fabric is an essential part of the decorating scheme used in a comfortable living room. The starkness of white walls and black accents is softened by splashes of sunlit yellow in a fabric that is also used for draperies. Quilted to cover the sofa and two of the chairs, the lovely print evokes a lyrical feeling that is complemented throughout the room by the crispness of checks covering the two easy chairs and the small stools.

Reupholstering with Latex

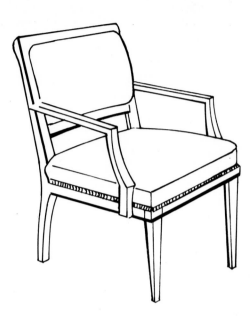

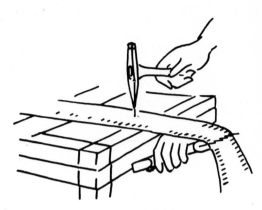

A webbing stretcher is a valuable tool that lets you put leverage on webbing to draw it tight. Buy a stretcher in a hardware store or make one yourself from scrap wood.

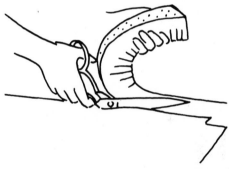

Stout scissors will cut 2-inch latex foam rubber cushions easily. Thicker cushions should be cut on a band saw. Many upholstery shops cut cushions to size from a pattern.

Apply two coats of rubber cement to both foam rubber and muslin, allowing the first coat to dry completely. When the second coat is tacky, join the two surfaces.

You can now handle tricky reupholstering jobs by taking advantage of modern materials and techniques.

New tools such as staple guns; new glues that grip like iron; rubber webbing that will bear any load; ready-to-use accessories such as casters, handles, and upholstery braid; paints in convenient spray cans—all help to make the job quicker, easier, and better looking.

One of the biggest helps to the amateur upholsterer is latex foam rubber cushioning. It is easy to handle and cut to shape, and eliminates wrestling with loose padding materials such as cotton or hair. Foam rubber is also very resilient, and thus makes one of the most comfortable seat-cushionings money can buy. Because of its resilience, it can even be used to replace steel springs, saving the time and trouble involved in tying a set of springs.

Place the cushion over the webbing and staple the muslin strips to the frame. If you want the cushion to have a rounded edge, pull down hard on the muslin and tuck the rubber under. It is easier to tuck in the foam rubber if you undercut it slightly as shown in the illustrations.

You are now ready for the upholstery fabric. Iron the fabric before you cover the chair, removing all creases.

Cut fabric to size. Double the edge under and tack in place, keeping it smooth and even. Make certain that you have the design properly centered and aligned before you start tacking. Tuck the corners in and, if necessary, sew them up. Add upholstery braid to hide tacks and rough spots; the braid can be attached with ornamental tacks or glue.

The total cost of reupholstering the chair shown in the illustrations was under $20, including the latex foam rubber, fabric, webbing, and upholstery braid.

A paper pattern of the chair seat is very handy, especially when the seat curves and cannot be measured accurately with a ruler. Use brown wrapping paper and a marking pen.

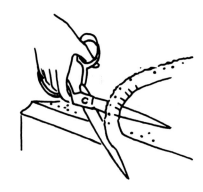

Undercut the cushion slightly if you want a rounded edge. The foam rubber is pulled down and tucked underneath to create a rounded edge that is solidly cushioned.

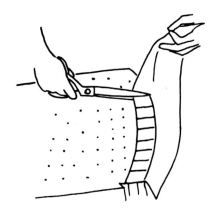

Cut V-shaped notches in the muslin if the cushion is curved, so that the cloth will lie flat on the cushion. The width of each notch depends on the sharpness of the curve.

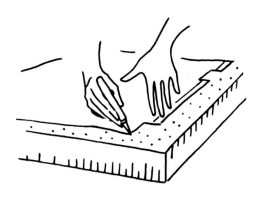

Allow an extra ½ inch all around when marking the pattern on the latex foam rubber. The extra rubber is compressed by the fabric and keeps the material trim and neat.

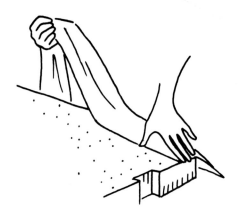

Plain muslin strips, rubber-cemented to the top of the cushion, are tacked to the chair frame to hold the cushion in place and help shape it. Pulling down rounds edge.

When the rubber cement is completely dry, place the cushion on the chair and tack or staple it to the frame. A staple gun is handy here because you use it with one hand.

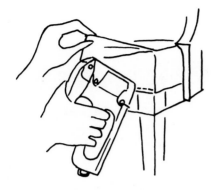

Making corners is not really hard. Pull the material around the corner, lift up the excess, and staple. Then pull the remaining cloth straight down and trim it to size.

Pull down on the muslin strip to give the cushion edge the degree of curve you want. Tuck extra cloth underneath and staple to the frame. Trim extra cloth with shears.

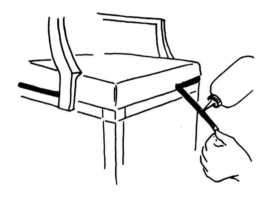

Cover with outer fabric and trim with a piece of upholstery braid or gimp to cover the staples. Run a bead of glue on the back of the braid, then press it in place.

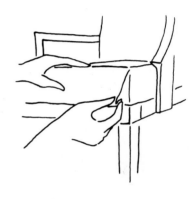

Fold the remaining edge underneath and tack or staple it in place. It may be necessary to sew the vertical slit shut. Use thread that matches the fabric and will not show.

feature inside construction of foam rubber instead of springs. The foam can be used directly over webbing, or it can be supported by a ¾-inch plywood board. Both methods work well since foam rubber is a lightweight material that comes in soft, medium, firm, and extrafirm densities. It is buoyant, holds its shape well, and, for those who are concerned, it is non-allergenic. Foam rubber is especially useful for amateur reupholstering projects that require replacement of springs and padding materials.

The final upholstery covering is applied by stretching the fabric tightly over the muslin and tacking it to the frame. Tacks with decorative heads may be used for this purpose, or you can work with ordinary upholstery tacks, concealing them with trimming when the job is done. To keep the stuffing from gathering dust or escaping, cover the webbing on the seat bottom with a closely woven and unobtrusive material: black cambric, for instance.

Cushions

The softest cushions for overstuffed chairs and sofas are made of a combination of down and feathers. The greater the proportion of feathers, the more the cushion will weigh. To prevent the down, which is very soft and fine, from working its way through the finished upholstery covering, down-and-feather cushions should always be made with an inner casing. The casing, usually of muslin, should be divided into three or four compartments to prevent the contents from shifting or bunching up in one place. For those to whom it is important that sofa and chair cushions always prevent a tidy appearance, it should be noted that down-and-feather cushions do not spring back to shape after having been sat upon. They do require being "puffed up" after use.

A cushion that will retain its shape, although it is not nearly as soft as down and feathers, is one that is made with inner springs. The spring units used for this purpose are made up of small springs, 2½ to 3 inches in diameter

and 3½ inches high. Each spring should be sewed into its own pocket in a casing made either of muslin or burlap. The springs should then be covered on all sides by several layers of cotton felt or thin layers of foam rubber. Since it is the seat that receives the greatest amount of wear in overstuffed furniture, the cushions should be reversible—cover them completely with the final upholstery fabric so they can be turned to distribute the wear on both sides.

Foam rubber has many advantages as both stuffing and cushion material. It can withstand hard usage, will not mat down or lump, retains its shape, and is a softer seat than inner springs (though not as soft as down and feathers). Foam rubber is also mildew- and mothproof. Cushions cut out of it may be covered with muslin before they are upholstered with the final fabric, but this is not absolutely necessary.

Knowing about the contents of your upholstered furniture and understanding how to put it together will help you to make wise choices when you are selecting new furniture. If you are considering undertaking a reupholstery project yourself, you will have a more accurate idea of what is really involved. In either case, how the furniture will look in the location you have planned for it is just as important as the soundness of its construction.

Choosing upholstery fabrics

Think of the walls and floor of the room as the background for your sofa or chair. The decorative fabric you choose should add interest to your room plan without overpowering or in any way detracting from the total effect. Upholstery

Warmth of color and richness of fabric make the comfortable-looking sofa a welcoming focal point for this living room. Surrounded by contrasts of color and texture, the strong pattern is pleasing without being distracting. Picking up the brown tone from the sofa, carpeting and draperies provide the background for a decorating plan that is elegant without being "stuffy."

The earthy green tones of a beautifully designed sofa are mixed with a hint of yellow. Combining the colors of nature's own palette, this fabric is a natural choice for a serenely monochromatic room. The very simplicity of the upholstery material is ideal for displaying the buttons and the handsome tufting that give the sofa its elegance.

1. To perk up your bedroom with a decorative uphol-stered headboard, as shown above, start with a panel of 1-inch plywood 6 feet high and 39 inches wide. Your lumberyard will trim the half-circle top. Next, pad the board with foam rubber; anchor with rubber cement.

2. Staple the upholstery fabric to the ply-wood panel, pulling the fabric as taut as possible and gathering the overlap evenly. It is easiest to start working up at the bottom point of the curve, finishing the top first and then working down the straight edges. Trim off excess fabric.

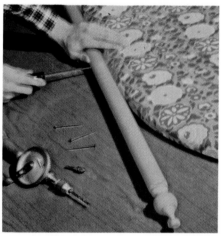

3. Posts are heavy curtain rods ornamented with turned finials; these are available at lumberyards or decorating stores. Drill holes near top and bottom of rods, and counter-sink screws through fabric into panel edge. Fill holes with putty and finish with paint.

4. To secure headboard to wall, mount angle brackets a little more than halfway up the panel. Fix a notched wood block to the wall and simply hook the brackets over it. This installation allows you flexibility to position the headboard 3 or 4 inches to either side.

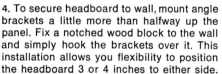

materials can help you to achieve a desirable variety in a number of ways. Color immediately comes to mind as a means of contrast; texture is another means, and so is the use of patterned fabrics in contrast to solids.

If your decorating scheme calls for a flowered wallpaper, for example, or a boldly patterned floor covering, it is best to choose solid-color upholstery fabrics. However, this cannot be termed a hard-and-fast rule. There is, today, a strong trend toward the eclectic feeling in decorating that favors many patterns, each almost fighting the others for attention. A pleasing variety can often be achieved by using tastefully harmonizing stripes or plaids to balance the plainness of solid-color upholstery and the busyness of patterned walls.

Practical appeal

Modern upholstery fabrics are available in a virtually unlimited variety of natural and man-made fibers, used singly or in combination. When choosing the decorative covering for your sofa or chair, look for the type of fabric that best suits the kinds of use your furniture will receive.

Some upholstery fabrics are made of 100% natural fibers—cotton, silk, wool, and linen. Sometimes they are woven into natural-fiber blends such as silk and wool, linen and wool, or cotton and silk. Fabrics are also made of natural fibers blended with man-made fibers in combinations like silk and rayon, cotton and polyester, or wool and nylon. Upholstery fabrics of such fibers as rayon, nylon, acrylic, or polypropylene are 100% man-made and are used either singly or in blends. In addition, you can cover upholstered pieces with vinyl, a material that simulates leather.

Whatever type of upholstery material you choose, check to be sure it has been treated with a soil-release finish. If it has not, inquire about having it treated because such protection is a significant contribution to the life and good looks of your furniture.

A careful distribution of fabrics and an imaginative selection of trimmings can give your room a feeling of unity in design. For example, if you are planning to put a sofa and two chairs in your living room, upholster both chairs (which need not be identical) in the same material, and cover the sofa in a fabric that is complementary in color and pattern. To emphasize the unity of the grouping, repeat the use of welting or fringes in the pieces that face each other.

Upholstering this chair is a salvage job well beyond the skill of a beginner. The modified wings present the difficulty, since they must be upholstered separately from the rest of the unit. The result, however, is a sprightly comeback for the chair that is definitely worth the effort.

◄ A home reclamation project rescued this old hospital bed from the junk heap and transformed it into a charming little sofa. A simple welding job lowered the headboard, giving the unit its distinctive shape, and a mattress and foam rubber bolsters, covered in a lighthearted Art Deco print, completed the face-lift. Home projects such as this allow singles and marrieds just starting out to fill the furniture gap without overstepping their budgets.

In this sleekly decorated little room, the showpiece, an elaborately tufted and corded small-scale sofa, is upholstered in wipe-clean ice-white vinyl. Its companion piece, an antique bedstead with curlicue curves, has a mattress and bolsters covered in an equally easy-to-care-for paisley print. Both pieces add glamor to the room, their utilitarian upholstery material in no way detracting from the overall impression of elegance.

A Rundown on What You Need For Your Second Home

A successful vacation home offers the chance to let go, a change from the routine drudgery of everyday living. The harder one works at planning a vacation home, the more likely it will prove an enjoyable escape.

Choosing a locale

The first decision is where to build your retreat. If you are a beach lover, do you want a view of the dunes and the ocean as your front yard, or would a cottage in the scrub pine woods half a mile from the shore please you more? Is a rocky site beside a stream the perfect setting, or would a cabin be your preference, as deep into the woods as a Jeep can go? Is a ski lodge worth the extra money for winterizing? Do you prefer a place on a southern waterway where a

boat slip can be built under your house? The decision is not entirely a rational one. People tend to build vacation homes where their hearts have led them many times before, such as

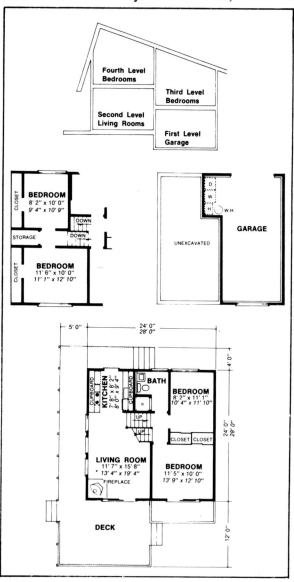

The flexible split-level offers a popular solution to a limited lot where the expansion must be vertical instead of horizontal. Layering rooms instead of spreading out means greater economy in several ways: less foundation and roofing is needed; plumbing lines can stack up and be shared; rooms insulate each other and save on heating and/or cooling costs. A split-level is especially suited to a sloping lot. In this design, the garage occupies the first level, while the second is devoted to both indoor and out-door living space consisting of kitchen, living-dining room with prefabricated fireplace, and a deck on three sides. Up half a level are two bedrooms and a bath; and the top floor can either become an additional pair of bedrooms, another bedroom and bath, or can be left open over the living room for a dramatic two-story effect. Appropriate to any vacation setting, whether in the woods or at the shore, the house is made of a combination of woods, with the emphasis on plywood. Siding is grooved, slightly tex-tured plywood with brightly painted overlaid accent panels, also of plywood. Plywood construction in floors and walls also helps hold down costs and, where left exposed, brings visual vitality. Structural timbers such as joists and rafters are stained and kept in sight both for economy and for their pleasant, rugged effect. The stairs, open and riser-less, harmonize with the rustic but contemporary mood.

rented cottages and areas seen on bicycle trips or on picnics. But, as in any other emotional decision, selecting a vacation site should be subject to some practical scrutiny.

Test the traveling time

Traveling time is as important a factor to consider as a vacation home's aesthetic values. The length of time it will take to go from your permanent home to your vacation house should be calculated. Many people find a four-hour drive the outside limit for regular weekend residency. Often a two-hour drive practically doubles on Friday and Sunday evenings, so it would be wise to try your projected drive during those hours at the height of the season. If you are aware of impending highway improvement,

A wooden wigwam would look at home on any wooded site, and expresses vacation spirit in its every aspect. The house is like an A-frame, an economical structure in that its walls are its roof. Timbers (like tepee poles) are set in a circle and meet at the top. Two-inch decking covers them, with hand-split shakes over all. The floor plan is actually octagonal. Each side is 12 feet long; each support timber is 32 feet long and is at its base 32 feet from its opposite timber, lending a visually satisfying symmetry to the design. On the first floor is the private master bedroom and bathroom, open living-dining and kitchen space leading to a deck and centering around a fireplace. Three living-dining walls are straight up to allow headroom and are roofed by the upper deck.

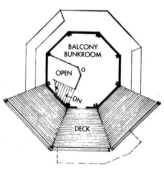

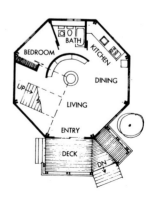

you cannot necessarily count on greater speed; increased traffic volume usually appears on new roads, and a bottleneck can take years to iron out. Train or bus travel is, of course, easier to check.

Choosing a lot

Once the locale is determined, you must choose the individual lot. How do you make an evaluation? Here are some checkpoints:

■ Financial aspects: what is the price? What is the down payment and what will interest be on further payments? What is the assessed value? Are there any back taxes or unpaid assessments?

What are the taxes and is an increase likely? Are any new assessments in the offing?

■ Legal aspects: is the title clear? How do zoning laws affect the type of house you have in mind? Does zoning protect the area against future crowding or commercial encroachments?

■ Physical aspects: is the lot size, shape, and slope adequate for the privacy and kind of structure you want? Is the drainage good? Will the soil suit your gardening plans? Are there some good trees that your builder can preserve? Is there a pleasant view?

■ Neighborhood: are the surrounding properties pleasant to be near? Is shopping available?

Concentric squares set at half right angles to each other produce a fascinating contemporary house with many conveniences. The largest square is the roof, the next largest the walls of the house swung around 45 degrees so that the roof overhangs all sides. The overhang shelters a carport, a deck, and anything else the owners like: a boat or a garden supply depot. The third square is small and parallel to the roof edges (indicated in blue on the plan). Here is the loft, with additional sleeping space for four children or two adults, offering views in all directions and a splendid perch for a solitary den. A master bedroom and two bunk rooms are separate and private, but the dining, living, and cooking areas are open to each other and to the triangular deck that provides space for varied family amusements and all sorts of entertaining. In this pared-down plan, one need not bother with superfluous housekeeping. The building materials, too, were planned for minimal upkeep: roof of plywood sheets coated with a polyvinyl fluoride film, exterior walls of textured plywood needing nothing after the initial coat of stain.

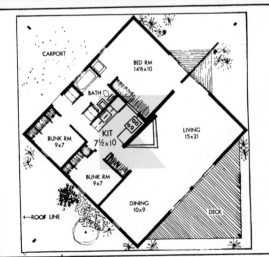

Are there recreation areas nearby and places of worship? Is there adequate medical care?

■ Public utilities and services: is there good public water or have your neighbors been able to reach good well water easily? How is sewage handled? Are electricity, gas, and telephone services reasonable to obtain? How good are fire and police protection? How is trash handled? What kind of road will you have and will the county maintain and clear it of snow?

■ Environment: is the area free of noise, air, and water pollution? Is the local government interested in preventing pollution? What is the climate of your particular area? Within a few miles there can be foggy and fog-free land, breezy and extremely windy sites. Are insects a problem?

■ Lawyer services: buying land and building a house require the services of a lawyer. There are contracts with the landowner, the architect, and the contractor. If you buy a prefabricated house you also need a lawyer. You may think you can manage these affairs on your own, but if you run into acts of bad faith, or even innocent muddles, you may find yourself over your head in legal complexities.

Where to find information on available land
There are many sources for answers about the locale. Your own observations should be augmented by interviews with the real estate agent, town clerk, prospective neighbors, and the local bank. If you can look at the land during or just after a heavy rain you may save yourself an unpleasant surprise. In fact, you should observe the area in all seasons before committing yourself to living there for a third of the year.

Special problems with beach houses
Look at building materials in terms of the damage that salt air, chronic damp, and constant sand will inflict. There is a windward side and a leeward side to a seashore house. You will want your exterior doors, terraces, and decks on the lee if possible, or sheltered by wind screens if they are to windward. The western

This bungalow-type compact house, a manufactured product with prefabricated components, can be erected in your favorite beach or lake area, and packs many rooms into its square shell: four bedrooms, living room, kitchen-dining room, two baths, a screened back porch, and a roofed but open-sided entry deck. Plan efficiency and low-cost detailing keep the price in line, but materials are sturdy, long-lasting, and upkeep is low. Both the front, with its entry deck, and the back, with its 10x23-foot screened porch, are attractive and a definite asset on sites where guests may approach from either side. Although this is a one-story design, its roof lifts at either end of the central living space to bring sun and sky into view through high glass gables. The living and kitchen-dining areas appear to be one, but a tall divider screens the workaday clutter from guests.

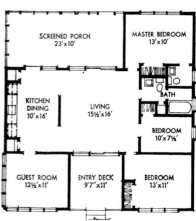

Three A-frame sections joined in a Y plan on a fairly flat and open site offer many luxuries of living both for a family and for parties. One A is all living room, two stories high, with a fireplace and the largest adjacent deck. The two other legs of the house contain on two floors a kitchen-laundry, dining room, four bedrooms, two bathrooms, and a deck off every room but the baths. All A-frames share certain advantages: the economy of a single roof and wall element, a wealth of storage space on the sides, and the great durability of the form in the face of snow loads and extreme winds. Except possibly for the trim, no part of the exterior needs any maintenance.

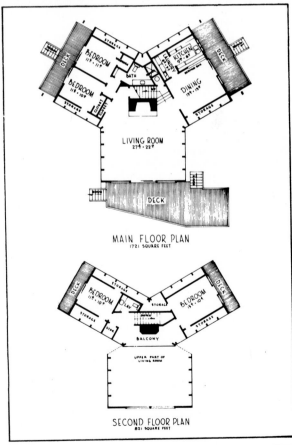

sun is particularly brilliant when reflected on the water, so think before you place many windows on that side. Storms and high seas are a threat best dealt with by good structural engineering.

Special problems of ski houses

Snow is the reason for the existence of this retreat, and its enemy. The roof and walls have to be able to carry a heavy load. If the area is deep snow country, an entrance door on the second floor is a sensible convenience instead of tunneling out from below. If your home is situated on the side of a mountain, a snowslide can

A compact yet expansive-looking one-story house was designed for year-round living in a wooded (possibly lakeside) vacation area. Oriented so that the view side is nearly all insulated glass, it expands to decks on both long flanks for a full day of sunny outdoor living. The living-dining room has three exposures and centers around a fireplace. The compact kitchen has a one-wall work area facing a recessed refrigerator. It is isolated by a partition that conceals the inherent disorder of cooking but lets the cook share the socializing taking place in the living-dining room. There are two full bedrooms, a double-bunk room, and a bath. The attractive, low, balanced roof appears to float above the high fixed-glass sections in the gable ends and under the eaves. The grooved siding that sheathes the house also appears on the interior, compounding the blending of outdoors and indoors. Other sophisticated rustic details include the exposed decking ceiling and exposed posts.

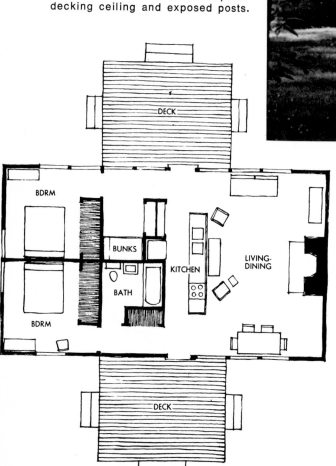

damage it. To prevent this, present the narrow side to the potential avalanche and give the structure secure underpinnings.

Special problems of desert houses

Check flash flood records in the locale and be sure not to place your house where they have occurred. Insulate as thoroughly as possible and air condition, or cross ventilate with windows. Deep eaves should be provided to keep out the sun, and shade must be planned for a deck or terrace. Remember that desert sun is hard on paint. A natural exterior surface such as brick, adobe, stucco, or wood is best.

Do you want a year-round retreat?

There is no reason not to plan for a year-round accommodation. Vacation spots out of season can sometimes offer inconveniences, particularly

for weekenders, but if the permanent inhabitants can surmount these difficulties, there is no reason why with adequate planning you cannot. Many people make the mistake of beginning their two-house existence thinking that they will visit their vacation home only for the skiing season or in the summer. Soon they start stretching the official season at both ends. Often the vacation house was not adequately equipped for such semipermanent residency and is lacking insulation, heating facilities, or a cooling system. It is wise therefore to look ahead when you build and include these essentials. The cost of their initial installation will be only a small fraction of the building bill, but installed separately at a future date these items might amount to much more. Remember, too, that, even if you only live in the house part of the year, you may rent it during the other seasons.

Where And How

Now that you have decided upon your type of house and its general location, you must get down to more specific problems.

Placing the house

The placement of the house is an important decision in which you, your architect, and your contractor should consider privacy, access, view, prevailing wind, snow loads, slope, unique characteristics such as a glacial boulder or a brook, existing vegetation, and family habits. Orientation to the sun is very important.

Rules regarding orientation

■ Bedrooms: bedrooms should face north if possible to keep them cool in summer, even though this makes them colder in winter. Bedrooms do not need much sunlight.

■ Living areas: family areas should face the east, which offers cheerful light but not the long hot rays of a setting sun.

Planned with four bedrooms for a big family, this is a clever design for a narrow lot with a slope. Although it is only 24 feet wide, it compensates in levels and length. In addition to the bedrooms, each with closet and one with a deck, are two full bathrooms, a separate kitchen and laundry, a dining room overlooking a living room, a deck on the lowest level, and a carport. The living room's fireplace is placed in a corner so that it faces in two directions and interferes as little as possible with wall space. The master bedroom and living room decks are both roofed. Plywood siding was used for the exterior and the texture runs horizontally to give an illusion of length. To fit a wooded slope, the living room and its deck are stepped down but, on a flat site, the entire floor can be level.

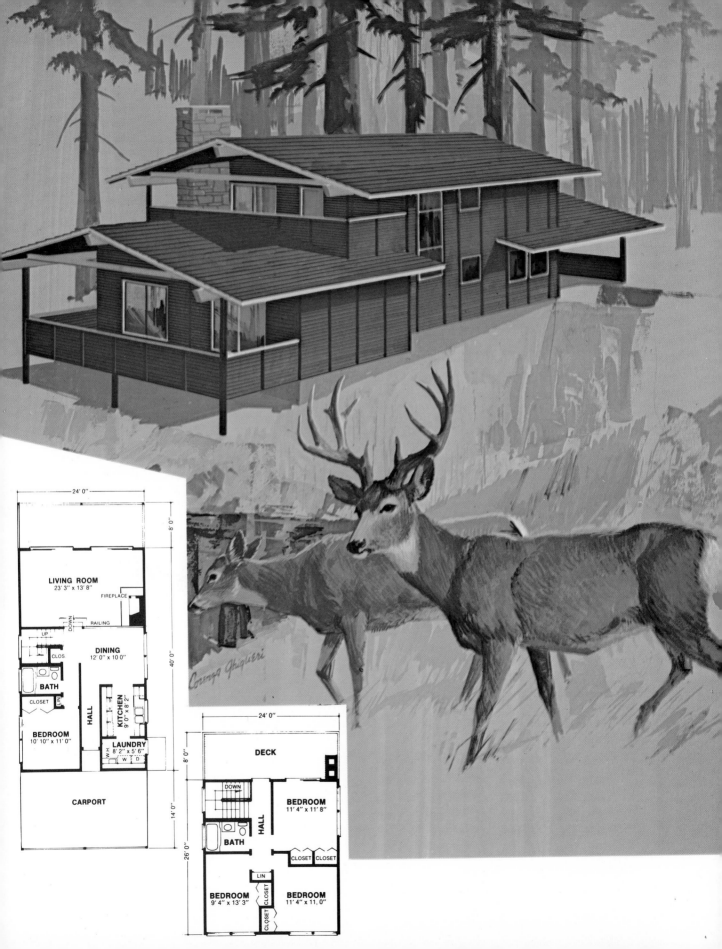

LIVING ROOM
23' 3" x 13' 8"

FIREPLACE

24' 0"

8' 0"

DOWN

RAILING

UP

CLOS

DINING
12' 0" x 10' 0"

BATH

LIN

HALL

KITCHEN
9' 0" x 8' 2"

CLOSET

40' 0"

BEDROOM
10' 10" x 11' 0"

LAUNDRY
8' 2" x 5' 6"

WH

W   D

CARPORT

14' 0"

24' 0"

8' 0"

DECK

DOWN

BEDROOM
11' 4" x 11' 8"

BATH

HALL

CLOSET   CLOSET

LIN

26' 0"

BEDROOM
9' 4" x 13' 3"

CLOSET

CLOSET

BEDROOM
11' 4" x 11' 0"

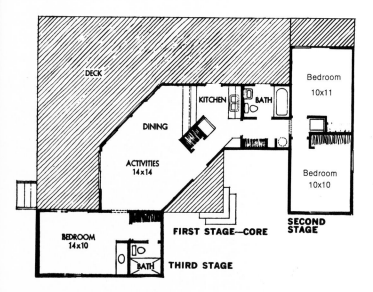

DECK

KITCHEN   BATH

Bedroom
10x11

DINING

ACTIVITIES
14x14

Bedroom
10x10

FIRST STAGE—CORE

SECOND STAGE

BEDROOM
14x10

BATH   **THIRD STAGE**

Preplanned for expansion, this prefabricated house is more deck than interior in its first, central, core version. The core is a blunted L-shape that includes living-dining room (a daybed provides sleeping space), kitchen, bath, storage. Almost every part of this beginning element opens or looks out on deck area where much of vacation living takes place. A portable fireplace on the deck extends its season. At one end of the core, a second-stage pair of bedrooms and more deck at the rear is added. Later a master bedroom and second bath hitches on. Each addition, which is incorporated when the budget and family needs dictate, enhances the privacy of the entrance and of the big deck behind. The initial accordion-fold roof becomes even more interesting as the wings are added. The interior ceiling reflects the roof line and its beams are painted brightly to emphasize the lines. The ceiling and walls are covered in the same paneling, a low-maintenance ploy that lends warmth and a sense of amplitude to the room. The same cedar-shingle roofing and reverse board-and-batten stained-plywood siding clothe the additions as well as the core, giving a unity to the whole. Naturally you can build the whole complex at once.

■ Kitchen: in a temperate zone, windows facing south or east have the best exposure for good light with no western slanting rays. In hotter climates, the southern sun may be too hot and a northern exposure would be better.

■ Glass walls: throughout most of the country, a southern exposure is the best direction for any room with large glass expanses, since the winter sun will offset any heat loss through the glass. Midday midsummer sun will not heat the room greatly since the sun is high at this time. In more tropical climates, reverse the orientation and let the biggest glass areas face north.

■ Bathrooms, utility rooms, garage: a western view is acceptable for strictly utilitarian rooms and they also provide a barrier between the late afternoon sun and the living areas.

Staking out the house

Staking out the house means driving markers into the earth where you expect the building corners to be, then running string from stake to stake to represent the walls as indicated in the blueprint. This gives you an idea of how the building will stand on the lot and what you

will see. This preliminary planning stage is a helpful form of research that often pays off.

Who will design your house?

If you can afford the cost and want your house to be custom-designed, you will want to hire an architect. There are numerous ways to find plans that are less expensive but designed by professional architects. Many people are satisfied with houses that builders produce without professional design work. Plans such as those included in this article can be purchased with working drawings and specifications. Other plan sources are magazines, lumber dealers, and manufacturers of building components. If you buy a manufactured or prefabricated house you contract not only for the plans but for delivery of the partially assembled parts.

Choosing an architectural style

As in choosing a location, the style of your home is an emotional decision. The style feels right or it does not. Past associations have created your preferences. One mistake is to choose a style without trying all that are available. A good preliminary step is to adopt the Sunday hobby of visiting as many model homes as you can. Your response to a style you had not considered may give you the answer, and a negative response to what you thought you liked may change your mind.

Vacation houses fall roughly into two categories: the rustic and the contemporary. Within these categories there are many designs, and the categories sometimes overlap. Keep in mind that vacation houses are especially designed for lighthearted living and minimal housekeeping, so you will not be shown any English Tudor or French manor houses.

Who should supervise the construction?

The architect will decide with you, as part of the contract, who will supervise the construction. If you are buying a house from a local builder, he, or someone with whom he is associated, will

For a luxury-loving couple, this Y-shaped hideaway with only one bedroom nevertheless contains three fireplaces, two baths, and a separate laundry room. Beautifully designed in the Frank Lloyd Wright spirit which mates a structure to its site, the building is dark brown wood inside and out to blend with earth and tree bark, and the fireplaces are faced with native stone. A spring-fed trout pond was part of the magic of the mountain site and the sun deck is cantilevered over the pond. A narrow deck runs almost entirely around the outer perimeter of the building. Even the roofing, asphalt and gravel, blends with the scene. Construction is post and beam with vaulted ceilings in a light tone contrasting with darkly stained structural members. Interior walls have mahogany paneling; exterior surface is weathered cedar vertical board and batten. One leg of the Y is the living room with a sliding glass wall on the deck that fills the V-shape. The leg opposite contains kitchen and serving space. The third leg contains the master suite and at the inner intersection of the three wings is a study separated from the living area by a tall bookshelf unit.

contract and supervise the work. Since it is highly unlikely that you can check the building of a vacation home daily, you have to choose your builder carefully. Ask to see finished products and make an effort to interview some of his former clients when not in his presence. If you are using purchased plans, your builder search must be equally careful. Buyers of custom-built houses, even if they plan to do some of the work themselves, usually have to employ experts for excavations, foundations, masonry, plumbing, and electrical work. The buyer can rarely oversee it all himself. Prefabs are usually sold by local builder-dealers, who oversee their own crews.

A general rule to keep in mind is that the supervisor in charge of the workmen on your house and the contractor responsible for the quality of the materials and the workmanship should sign a lawyer-drawn contract with you. Your lawyer should have done this kind of work before. Not only does a contract protect you, but it convinces the builder you expect a good job.

Prefabricated homes

A prefabricated or manufactured home is one purchased from a manufacturer who contracts to deliver to your site floors, roof, and walls, both exterior and interior, and the windows and doors. These elements have been factory produced in modules in readiness for construction, in contrast with more conventional homes that are put together on the site piece by piece. The local seller is a dealer-builder whose crew is ready to assemble the modules. Local masons, plumbers, and electricians are not necessarily part of his crew. Prefabricated home buyers also receive contracts. Have your lawyer read yours before you sign it. What you may believe to be a promised wood floor may actually be, in tiny print, bare concrete.

Price comparisons

Manufactured houses are no cheaper than conventional homes. What can make them a good buy, however, is that you are purchasing an architect's design for less than a private de-

signer's fee. In addition, you get guaranteed high-quality materials and a reliable assurance that the builder will make good on defects. You also save on on-the-site labor charges because the factory work, included in the price, has been done on an assembly line at lower unit cost. Building time is often as much as a month less than construction of a standard structure.

Time needed to build a vacation home
A vacation home will require as much time to construct as a year-round house. If you want to move in by summer, start construction after the preceding summer, have it closed in by winter, and finish the decorating in the spring.

Room-by-Room Suggestions

Although most of the principles of building, furnishing, and decorating apply for vacation homes as much as for your regular home, there are special hints that can be of value.

Bedrooms and bathrooms
Keep in mind, when planning space, that families grow in size. Children may turn the day-to-day residence into an empty home when they marry, but each marriage means an additional young person when vacation time arrives. Not

Shaped like the lower half of an A-frame, this cleverly planned house displays many of the advantages and few of the problems of the usual A-frame. Pluses: sloping walls and roof are designed to shed snow and shrug off winds; glass end walls for light and view; compact, uncomplicated construction. Minuses avoided: no waste-space peak, no steep sides that cramp rooms, no tiny second floor. In this full two-story plan, three upstairs bedrooms, one for bunks, can handle a proper houseful. Downstairs, on the sloping site, one end deck juts over a hillside, the other lies flat. On a flat site, both decks would cover the ground. Especially different is the living room, which contains a recessed fireplace, built-in sofa, and deeply carpeted pit. For a more conventional seating area, the large zone marked "DINING" is also available, in addition to generous outdoor living space on both decks. Roof walls are shingled.

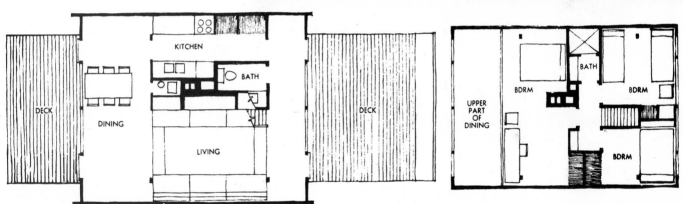

to mention the offspring! Therefore, build as many bedrooms as you can manage, and a bathroom for every two bedrooms. It does not matter if the bedrooms are small, since bunk beds are fine for holidays and are wonderful space savers even though they are difficult to make up.

Built-ins keep bedrooms tidy

Vacation-house bedrooms require only enough room for the beds, moving-around space, and storage. If you can build drawer storage under the beds or into closets, instead of having to leave space for dressers, you will have saved that many square feet and have one less item to dust and wax.

Kitchen planning

The kitchen in a vacation house should be carefree. In the kitchen, you want storage for a lot of food, including the frozen variety, a machine to do the dishes, and a lot of built-in socializing for the cook. This means a window to look out of, if possible, and fairly easy access to the living room. Most vacation-house designs have taken care of this by opening the kitchen to the living-dining area. The only divider is likely to be a snack bar or serving counter.

A vacation kitchen can be small, as many efficient kitchens are. Study the article on *Kitchens* (Vol. 10, p. 1860; and Vol. 11, p. 1923) and make sure efficiency is built into the plan.

A three-decked chalet with Alpine details does not waste an inch of space. Two-story living room with fireplace opens to a kitchen whose snack bar also serves as a buffet counter. Balcony over the living room is both stair landing, possible storage place, and romantic perch with a view through the wide living room windows. Each upstairs bedroom opens to the railed upper deck. On the lower floor, decks at each end are useful not only for outdoor living but for stacking wood, and handling boots and skis. Exterior is all wood, interior is paneled.

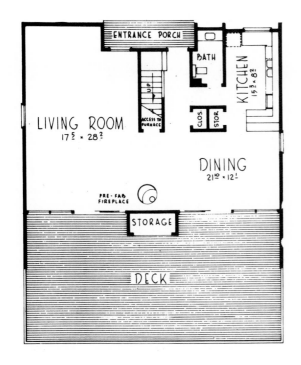

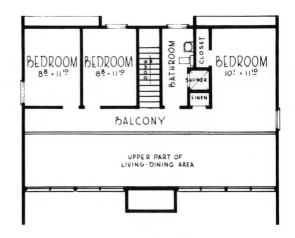

Solid and symmetrical, with unique dormers, this contemporary design has front and back entrances. The larger rear deck is railed, flanked by wind breaks that are side wall extensions, and includes a versatile storage center between the long sweeps of glass. The living room reaches up two stories, overlooked by a balcony that adjoins a bath, two private bedrooms, and one open bunk room. There is another bath downstairs, a kitchen open to the dining part of the big living area, and a fireplace.

Plan for a laundry

If you ask enough women, you might find that half of them would give up a dishwasher for a washing machine. Sacrifice part of a bathroom or even a whole closet, but make an effort to include a home laundry or at least a washer when you build.

The vacation-house bathroom

For the vacation home, consider the new pre-fabricated fiber-glass-reinforced plastic bathroom that is small and rapidly installed. An outside shower, even a cold one, particularly in a beach home, is a great help in keeping floors clean. In a heavily populated house, consider installing extra wash basins in bedrooms, bunkrooms, or even the regular bathrooms to help prevent boardinghouse lineups. Study the article on *Bathrooms,* Vol. 3, p. 398.

How to estimate water heater size

For vacation houses, plumbers recommend a storage water heater of the fast-recovery type to provide water soon after arrival from the city. A family of four with two bathrooms, a laundry, and a dishwasher can manage with a 50-gallon heater. If the family is larger or if guests are frequent, get a larger-capacity heater.

Vacation-house living space

Few vacation houses afford space both for a formal living room and an easygoing family room, so you have to combine elements of the two. The emphasis should be on the informal side since vacationers seldom expect elegance. However, there will be situations where a family will want to entertain formally, observing amenities with seating arrangements in conversation groups, a handy table for every guest, lighting that is flattering and easy on the eyes, and traffic patterns without dead ends and bottlenecks. In such cases, the bigger the room, the easier it will be to arrange for this. If you have to cut costs, do it in a way that will not force you into too small an entertaining area. Having the living room open to the dining space is a good way to make them both larger, and vacation gregariousness seems to dictate that the kitchen also open to this space.

The fireplace

A vacation home and a fireplace form a nearly inseparable combination. The only vacation-house owners who do not have fireplaces are those who are figuring out how to add one. A full masonry fireplace adds about $1,000 to the cost of a house. A prefabricated metal model costs far less and the wonderful sights, sounds, and smells of burning logs are equally enjoyable.

The designs of prefabricated fireplaces offer a wide variety of styles from which to choose.

Decks and terraces for outdoor living

One reason to build a vacation house is to enjoy outdoor living, and the placement of the terrace or major deck may dictate the way the house sits on its site. If you will have a single deck or terrace for all your family needs, make it as big as an indoor family room and, if possible, build it on the south side to catch the sun all year. Other considerations enter into the choice, such as views and prevailing wind. Depending on the climate, you may want a permanent roof, perhaps a wood or metal grid on which to train vines, or an awning that you can roll and unroll. The presence of some well-established trees on your site, particularly if they are shade trees, may be one of the deciding factors in the location and design of your deck.

This one-story, redwood, manufactured home can be finished by two carpenters in two weeks. The prefabricated parts come precut and drilled, and the package is complete except for foundation, plumbing, heating, and electrical wiring. Surrounded by deck on three sides, the plan is the usual vacation-house open system, and the two bedrooms share a bath between. On one long side, the wall is blank below but opened by a long dormer to sun and sky. View side of the living room is an expanse of windows. The building is faced inside and out with walls made of tongue-and-groove-finished redwood boards, both walls nailed to the studs simultaneously from the outside. Both walls are prefinished, which means that no painting, staining, or trimming is required.

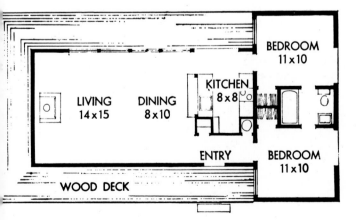

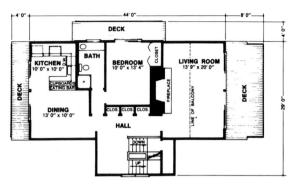

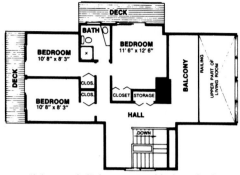

Intersecting modified A-frame shapes join together to create a luxurious year-round lodge for a mountain site. Although tall and expansive, the house calls for plywood construction techniques that keep building costs and maintenance moderate. Entry is planned from the sheltered carport at ground level, where are also a central heating plant and generous storage space. The second, or main, level contains the most floor space and includes separate living and dining rooms, kitchen, bath, and bedroom well insulated for privacy by closets and other buffering spaces. Bedroom, dining, and living rooms each open to a railed deck. The third floor contains a balcony overlooking the living room (big enough to take a few young people with sleeping bags on a big ski weekend), three bedrooms and another bath. Each room has access to the deck. A log-sized fireplace is a focal point.

If you can afford to build more than one deck or terrace, you might want to construct one of these: a tiny secluded deck for sunning outside a bedroom or bathroom; a children's play deck handy to the kitchen and equipped for their needs; an eating deck shaded and screened and close to the kitchen.

Choosing materials: siding

The exterior siding for vacation homes is usually made of wood, either boards or shingles, shakes (longer and heavier shingles), or varieties of plywood. The finish may be reapplied or done after construction, and it might be a stain or a paint. One problem with paint is that it leads, after a few years, to more painting. Many houses do very well simply left to weather and mellow. Among the popular new siding materials available are aluminum, vinyl, fiber glass, and steel, finished to resemble a new paint job and practically maintenance free. In hot climates, concrete block is very popular because it is cool, termite-resistant, and relatively impervious to storms. Architects are beginning to experiment with new inexpensive masonry techniques such as Gunite sprayed on metal lath.

Choosing materials: roofing

Asphalt roll roofing is an inexpensive material, cheaper but less attractive than asphalt shingles, which comes in a variety of colors and shapes. Built-up roofing is made of layers of fiber glass or felt and asphalt. The top layer is asphalt covered with gravel or chips of stone and is applied to flat or low-pitched roofs. Clay tile is expensive roofing but is often dictated by a tropical climate. Cedar, cypress, or redwood shingles or shakes are a favorite with both traditional and contemporary designers and they have a 30-year life expectancy.

Choosing materials: interior walls

Probably the most popular interior wall finish is gypsum board that has been taped, spackled, and painted or papered. You cannot go wrong with such a wall, although for a vacation house you may be interested in a woody look. Old-fashioned solid wood paneling and plywood paneling in a large variety of woods and prices are easily available. Of all the woods obtainable, plywood is far cheaper than solid lumber, and you can buy it prefinished. Hardboard also comes prefinished in many styles and it is equally tough and modestly priced. Laminated plastic bonded to a flakeboard base also forms a good wall, especially for a kitchen, bathroom (including the tub recess), or a nursery. Joints between panels cannot be concealed and are usually covered with flat battens, half-rounds or other wood molding, or with strips of aluminum. You can also apply floor tiles such as cork, vinyl, and linoleum to a wall, or even carpet a wall.

Choosing materials: flooring

If you want an easily maintained or no-care floor, do not use pine or fir where the floor will be bare, since soft wood wears badly. Try a No. 1 common oak or other hardwood that will not be uniform (compared with clear or select grades) but which will not dent, scuff, and lose its finish like a soft wood.

Wall-to-wall carpeting over plywood is cheaper than installing a hardwood floor (unless you choose a luxury carpet) and is a good idea for vacation-house bedrooms except in sandy areas. Cover plywood with sisal or tatami matting as another solution. Leaving the concrete slab uncovered is perfectly satisfactory for some people if they paint it a pretty color, and it is a real treat if someone knows how to stencil on designs. There is a huge list of resilient-sheet and resilient-tile floor coverings to consider: vinyl, cork, linoleum, vinyl-asbestos, rubber, and asphalt (see *Resilient Floor Covering,* Vol. 15, p. 2786). If you dislike cleaning often, try to choose flooring that still looks good when it is slightly dirty. Ceramic tile, especially in terracotta color, is easy to maintain, as is brick, but they cost a mason's price.

Cost-cutting

It is possible to save money on materials. Certain items are inexpensive because they do not have to be shipped, such as local stone, adobe in the southwest, and local brick. Other materials are inexpensive anywhere, such as asphalt roofing and concrete block. Some components require minimal labor to handle, thus cutting labor costs, such as plywood siding and roofers, prefabricated bathrooms and fireplaces. Labor costs can be cut when items are bought prefinished at the factory, such as wall paneling and aluminum siding. Lumberyards sell many stock items, like mantels, wall storage units, and pilasters and pediments, all of which save you the cost of custom millwork.

Decorating a vacation house: spiritual liberation

Decorating a vacation house can be approached from two directions: as a contributor to the holiday mood, and as a means of controlling maintenance chores. What spells holiday to one family will leave another cold. The general rule that applies to all families is to create a change from whatever style you are enjoying in the city. Country corny may be a delightful switch from sleek urban Bauhaus for some; for others, chrome and plastic modern at the beach might be what city French Provincialists yearn for. A change in color is part of the uplift of moving from one place to another. Red, white, and blue at the lakeside is half the lifestyle; a beige, brown, and naturals home the other.

Housekeeping liberation

You can do a minimum of cleaning and refurbishing anywhere, but especially in your vacation home. Throughout this article emphasis has been on easy-care planning and materials. Essentially the idea in vacation-home decorating is to use fabrics that get dirty very slowly or clean quickly or both: vinyl-coated wallpaper, vinyl dining-chair seats, dirt-proofed upholstery fabrics, indoor-outdoor carpeting, sealed prefinished wall paneling, plastic-laminate counter- and tabletops, quick-sweep flooring, no-fuss drip-dry curtains (if any), and wipable tablecloths. It is hard to resist light colors for their cheerfulness, but choose those treated for imperviousness, or else those that are machine-washable and dryable.

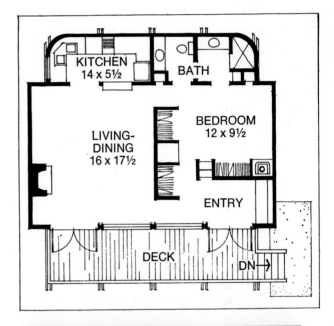

In a setting of beach plants, hot sun, and sand, this simple yet distinctive little cottage blends attractively with the natural landscape. The cottage is set on doubled 4x12 girders and concrete piers, sunk deep into the sand. A wall of windows faces the sea, letting in a flood of natural light that is augmented by a 4-foot celestory unit. High ceilings, overscaled twin chimneys, a sunscreen of extended roof beams, and a wide sun porch give the house a distinct personality. Inside there is ample space for comfortable vacation living with long 8-foot storage units dividing the living areas, and a huge fireplace to keep the cottage snug at night.

Recognize the Different Types And Know Their Beauties

Veneering is the art of applying thin layers of ornamental woods to furniture surfaces. The technique of veneering enables the skilled cabinetmaker to cover a framework or base of no extraordinary visual quality with a facade that is rich in color and patterned markings.

History

It was not until the seventeenth century that entire cabinet surfaces were covered with decorative veneering. During the Italian Renaissance, the related art of intarsia was a prominent feature of furniture design. Minute pieces of colored woods were combined and inlaid to form elaborate patterns and images of landscapes and figures. Ivory, metal, and bone were also used in this way. Such intarsia decorations were applied chiefly to lecterns, wood coffers, and choir stalls; simpler pieces of furniture were often embellished solely with inlaid borders.

In England, Queen Anne furniture was characterized by walnut veneers of remarkable beauty, and the use of brilliantly contrasting veneers became a hallmark of later-eighteenth-century cabinetwork. Veneered surfaces of satinwood and mahogany were inlaid with decorative borders whose patterns combined rosewood, tulipwood, satinwood, and mahogany. In America, the practice of veneering dates from the eighteenth century, and it was a principal feature of the Sheraton and Hepplewhite styles.

Decline and recovery

During the nineteenth century, when elaborate furniture decoration was in universal demand, certain manufacturers capitalized on the popular taste by gluing fine mahogany veneers over badly constructed pieces made from inferior woods. The veneers tended to wear badly and to chip and warp. Eventually, the term "veneering" took on the meaning of "disguise" —a false front masking a shoddy and corrupt interior. However, the genuine craft survived this unfortunate debasement; veneering is widely practiced and admired today.

Today's veneers

Veneer offers a number of advantages to furniture makers. It is the only method by which the grain of wood can be used for designs in panels or on wide surfaces. It is the only way, too, in which certain woods, which would warp if used in their solid state, can be worked. It reduces the cost of rare woods by increasing the amount of usable material, and permits the use of beautiful woods that are too fragile for structural purposes. Finally, far from masking weak or poorly made cabinetry, veneers achieved with modern lamination techniques actually increase the strength of furniture and help to preserve it.

Modern veneers are cut by machine in thicknesses that range from 1/50th to 1/100th of an inch. (Hand-cut veneers were rarely less than $\frac{1}{8}$ inch thick.) Such paperlike thinness makes it possible for contemporary furniture makers to lay veneers in double or triple layers, with one veneer lying across the grain of the one beneath. This technique virtually eliminates

A collection of wood carvings is displayed against walnut panels. The subtle interplay of wood surfaces and patinas is brilliantly set off by deep red walls. To achieve this luxurious effect, use prefinished random-grooved plywood panels with walnut veneer.

Types of Veneer Cuts

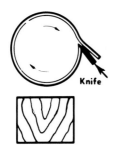

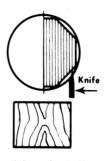

The manner in which veneers are cut is an important factor in producing the various visual effects obtained. Two logs of the same species, but with their veneers cut differently, will have entirely different visual characteristics even though their colors are similar. In veneer manufacture, five principal methods of cutting veneers are used.

In rotary cutting, the log is mounted centrally in the lathe and turned against a razor-sharp blade; separating the veneer is not unlike unwinding a roll of paper. Since this cut follows the log's annual growth rings, a bold variegated grain marking is produced. Rotary-cut veneer is wide.

In flat slicing, the half log, or flitch, is mounted with the heart side flat against the guide plate of the slicer, and the slicing is done parallel to a line through the center of the log, producing a variegated figure.

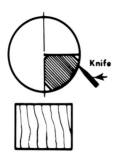

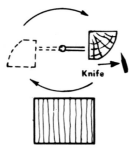

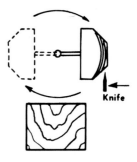

In quarter slicing, the quarter log is mounted on the guide plate so that the growth rings of the log strike the knife at approximately right angles, producing a series of stripes, straight in some woods and varied in others.

Rift-cut veneer is produced from the various species of oak. Oak has medullary ray cells that radiate from the center of the log like curved spokes of a wheel. The rift or comb grain effect is obtained by cutting at an angle of about 15 degrees off the quartered position to avoid the flake figure of the medullary rays.

Half-round slicing is a variation of rotary cutting—segments of the log are mounted off center in the lathe. This results in a cut slightly across the annual growth rings, and the visual effect modifies the characteristics of rotary and plain veneers.

warping, bulging, or chipping, and it produces veneers that resist severe climate or temperature changes and stand up well in steam-heated rooms. Veneers laminated in this manner are of greater beauty as well.

Woods, markings, and cuts

The wood most popular today, both for construction and for veneering, is mahogany. Other imported woods that are widely used for construction and veneers include rosewood, walnut, ebony, teak, and satinwood. American woods commonly used for veneers are redwood, ash, magnolia, cedar, elm, cypress, spruce, and beech. Woods used exclusively for veneers include amboyna, snakewood, yew, olive, kingwood, myrtle, acacia, laurel, box, and sandalwood.

All raw logs are characterized by annual rings and medullary rays. The rings and rays vary widely in size, arrangement, texture, and color,

Matching Effects

Book match. All types of veneers are used, and every other sheet is turned over just as are the leaves of a book. The back of one veneer meets the front of the adjacent veneer, producing a matching-joint design.

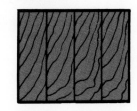

Slip match. Veneer sheets are joined side by side and give the effect of repeating the flitch figure. All types of veneers may be used, but quarter-sliced is most common.

Random-match veneers are joined with the intention of creating a casual unmatched effect. Veneers from several logs may be used in the manufacture of a set of panels.

Vertical butt and horizontal bookleaf match. When the height of a flitch is inadequate, veneers may be matched vertically as well as horizontally.

Special Matching Effects

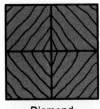

Diamond

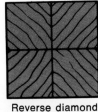

Reverse diamond

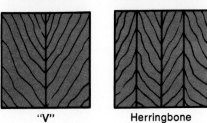

"V"

Herringbone

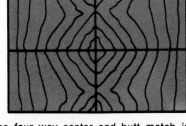

The four-way-center-and-butt match is ordinarily applied to butt, crotch, or stump veneers, since it is the most effective way of revealing the beauty of their configurations. Occasionally, flat-cut veneers are matched in this manner when panel length requirements exceed the length of the available veneers.

and these variations, almost infinite in their range, are what lend distinction to veneers. The annual rings comprise a silent history of all natural phenomena—rainfall, sunlight, soil fertility—that have contributed to the growth of the tree. Medullary rays are radial lines cutting across the annual rings.

In addition to the trunk of the tree, sources from which veneers are cut include the crotch, the butt or stump, and burls. The crotch is the point at which the tree forks into two limbs, and crotch veneers are characterized by a V-shaped grain, with markings described as plumes, feathers, or crossfire. Veneers cut from the butt or stump where the tree spreads horizontally towards its roots also yield a V-shaped figure, often with smaller cross rays or curls. A burl is a cluster of undeveloped limb buds shaped like a flattened hemisphere.

Plastic veneers

In recent years, the technique of veneering has been applied to man-made materials. Plastic laminates are available in very thin sheets with matching flexible edging. These veneers are applied with specially developed adhesives.

Cut the plastic veneer with a hand saw. The furniture piece to be covered should be cleaned of old oil, wax, and dirt. Apply the adhesive both to the bottom of the plastic veneer and to the top of the furniture surface. The adhesive bonds on contact, so place the veneer panel on the receiving surface with care. Apply pressure with a rolling pin or linoleum roller, paying particular attention to the edges. When the bonding is complete, trim rough edges and glue on edging or trim.

Loose or blistered veneers can also be repaired at home. If the veneer is loose at the edges, insert new glue, using a flat knife or a kitchen spatula. Protect the reglued area with heavy board or felt, and place weights over it until the glue dries. If the area to be repaired is in the center, slit the veneer along the grain, using a razor blade. Insert the glue, using a knife or spatula, and wipe off excess glue at once. Then protect the reglued area and weight it as before. Old glue should be removed with white vinegar, and the cleaned area must be allowed to dry thoroughly before regluing. Trim broken or damaged veneers to a regular shape and cut a new patch to fit exactly. Use wrapping paper to make a pattern before cutting the patch piece.

◄ Triple wood cabinets adorned with hammered bronze plaques and jewellike door pulls dominate this dining area. Skillfully applied veneers repeat patterns on each door, and the rhythm is refined by the subtle variations that wood grains always contain.

Wood grains are exquisitely matched in this storage-divider ensemble. When the drawer housing the stereo set is closed, the veneered front of the lower cabinet presents a flowing expanse of unbroken grain pattern. The mounted drop-leaf cabinet also features matching veneers that blend when the leaf is closed. Veneer-enclosed television set completes the group.

Effective Methods for Cleaning And Cooling the Air in Your Home

Proper ventilation in the home will not only make the occupants more comfortable, it will make the house easier to clean and at lower cost. Most homeowners are insufficiently aware of these important facts.

Smoke, dust, oil fumes from the furnace, grease fumes from the stove, and water vapor are constantly being generated in the house. The result is that the house takes on odors, while grease builds up on walls and appliances, especially in the kitchen, and time, energy, and costly detergents are necessary for periodic cleanups. It will never be possible to eliminate completely the smoke, dust, grease, and water vapor, but they can be reasonably controlled. Their volume can be reduced by removing impurities from the air close to their generating source, thus keeping the house cleaner and comparatively odor-free.

The way to do this is by a system of filtration or by periodically replacing the air in the house. In short, use proper ventilation.

Some of the bad side effects of poor ventilation, says the Home Ventilating Institute, are cracking wallpaper, peeling paint, warped and sticking doors, and the beginnings of mildew, dry rot, and dust in the basement or utility room because of too much humidity in the air.

According to university tests conducted by the Home Ventilating Institute, steam from showers and the bath will corrode metal bathroom fixtures, cause paint to crack and wallpaper to peel. Paint will even blister on the house exterior because of excess humidity in the interior. It is fact that today's washing machines will put about 5 pounds of water vapor into the home each week. The average American kitchen produces about 200 pounds of grease-filled air annually.

The solution to these irksome home ailments is to install a ventilating fan in such rooms as the kitchen, bathroom, utility room, and laundry room. The result will be a cleaner and more comfortable house to live in through the removal of steam, grease, cooking odors, and stale air.

Capacity of the ventilating fan

When buying a ventilating fan, it is important to get a unit for a specific job in a specific room. For example, if your bathroom has a 10x10-foot floor area with a 10-foot ceiling, it will have 1,000 cubic feet of air space. Standards set by the Home Ventilating Institute and the Federal Housing Administration state that the air in a bathroom should be circulated eight times in an hour. This means that a bathroom with 1,000 cubic feet of air space should be equipped with a 125-CFM fan. CFM refers to the cubic feet of air per minute moved by the fan. The CFM is obtained by dividing the 1,000 cubic feet of air space by eight, the number of times the air should be circulated in the bathroom each hour.

Standards of the HVI and the FHA state that the average air changes in a laundry room should be six per hour; fifteen air changes per hour are recommended for a hot and steamy kitchen.

Thus, when you buy a ventilating fan, you should know the CMF for the specific room in which it will be used. Consumer guides even recommend buying a fan with a slightly larger CMF than your requirements demand. Additionally, local code situations often dictate the required size.

Types of fans

There are two primary types of ventilating fans that you can buy to exhaust heat and humidity, odors, smoke, and grease from interior spaces:

■ Ceiling fan: an exhaust fan of this type is flush-mounted in the ceiling and requires minimal ductwork. The control switch, which can be a single- or multispeed unit, turns on the fan and exhausts the air through a wall cap or to the roof or attic space. In the case of its use in a bathroom, the fan can be purchased with a built-in electric heater in combination, plus a timer.

■ Sidewall fan: this fan exhausts the air from the interior space into a weatherproof hood on the exterior wall. Control is by a single- or multispeed switch on the wall.

Fan location

The fan, wherever it is used, should be placed as close as possible to the source of the air contamination. In a laundry center, the fan should be placed over and near the washer and dryer; in the kitchen, a hood fan would be located over the stove; in the bathroom, the fan would go on a wall or the ceiling, close by tub or shower.

Ductwork

When ductwork is installed for a ventilating fan of any type, it is important that the ducts be as straight as possible. If there are many bends or elbows in the ductwork, the amount of air that is exhausted is greatly reduced, lowering the efficiency of the system. Elbows, for example, can cut down on the exhaust emission of dirty air by as much as 20 percent.

Nonducted ventilators used in a kitchen over an oven or range hood are not as effective as ducted types. Nonducted fans will cut down on odors, grease, and smoke but cannot take heat or moisture from the air.

The best way to vent air from a fan is directly to the outside of the house. While air from such rooms as the bathroom or a laundry room can be vented into the attic if necessary, the kitchen fan is required to exhaust the air directly to the outside. The reason for this is that grease-laden air vented to an interior area of the house can be a fire hazard.

Attic fans

The first half of this article deals with exhaust fans that ventilate specific rooms of a house.

Another form of home ventilation, particularly important if you do not have central air conditioning, is through-the-house ventilation to exhaust hot air and draw in fresh air from outdoors. The most logical and effective location for such an exhaust fan is in the attic, although homes without attics can use a basement ventilation system.

In hot weather, the attic temperature can be as high as 130 degrees. Walls and ceilings absorb heat, and even cooler evening temperatures will not reduce room temperature appreciably. An attic fan can reduce the temperature as much as 27 degrees. However, if you use a fan to remove hot attic air, close off the attic or you may draw in hot air from the outside.

If you do not have general air conditioning, the next best aid to through-the-house comfort is adequate ventilation. To achieve good air circulation, a vented attic fan is the logical device, but not an absolute necessity. Without a fan, the vents carry the full work load. Good air circulation above the insulation will make your house more comfortable and aid in getting rid of moisture condensation. In the illustration, continuous, effective circulation has been achieved through screened and louvered gable and eave vents. Vents should have a ½-square-inch opening for each square foot of uninsulated attic space.

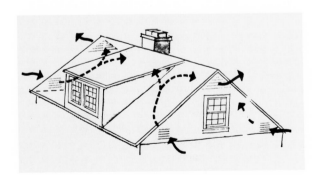

Sealed attic: if your living space extends to the attic, increased comfort can be achieved by installing a fan in partition between the living area and the unfinished section. Hot air is exhausted into eaves and out roof vent.

Unsealed attic: a home with an unsealed attic can best be ventilated by the installation of an airtight suction box over a ceiling grille. The fan, which is part of the unit, places positive pressure in the attic and forces the warm air through exhaust openings in the gables.

Basement: in a home without an attic, a basement ventilation system can be employed, but less effectively. Windows will permit adequate exhaust of hot air with the aid of a fan. In homes where there is both an attic and a basement, locate the ventilation system in the attic.

Shed-type roof: the diagram shows exhaust in a clerestory position under a slanted roof. However, under ideal conditions, the ventilating fan would function better if mounted on the flat area adjoining the shed roof. In the illustration, the projecting shed roof protects the fan and the metal louvers.

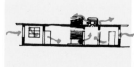

Flat roof: exhaust fans do not necessarily have to be installed in the attic. In a flat-roofed house, the fan can be installed at the roof line. The fan unit is protected by the metal-louvered cupola that is above the roof.

What size fan to get

Effective through-the-house air circulation is calculated in the same way circulation of specific room ventilators is measured—that is, in cubic feet per minute. To arrive at the correct figure, consider both the volume of the entire house, minus the attic, and the number of air changes per minute desired. One air change a minute is recommended throughout the United States. For example, if the total area of a house measures 35x25x8 feet, its volume would be 7,000 cubic feet (length x width x height). You would then know the fan must move 7,000 CFM. Read the fan information before purchase to find its CFM rating.

A choice of fan positions

An attic fan can be installed in a horizontal position on the upstairs ceiling, immediately above a ceiling grille, or standing vertically against an outside wall or gable of the attic. A third variation is to install the fan in a vertical position to the floor and connect it to a suction box.

The best location for an attic fan is in the center of the house in the upstairs ceiling if there are two levels. Make sure you do not restrict air flow to the fan. The overall capacity will be reduced if the fan is placed close to a wall or in a corner.

House roofs may vary in pitch, size, and airtightness. The following is a list of installation suggestions, depending on the size and layout of the house:

■ Single-story low-pitched roof: install the fan in the ceiling as near as possible to the center of the house. Place the exhaust louvers in the gable ends or in the soffit overhang if the house has a hip roof.

■ Two-story house—full attic and stairway: place a suction box (an airtight box surrounding the unit to prevent the fan from sucking in attic air as well) over stairway opening to attic. Air is sucked from stairwell and deflected into attic horizontally.

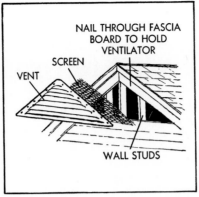

For homes with roof ventilation systems, adjustable gable louvers are available with telescopic blades that slide out to permit installation in either low- or high-pitched roofs. Louver blades expand from both sides to increase triangle size. Bugs are kept out with a plastic screen that fits behind louver.

Ventilator installation: illustration shows how ventilator is put into gable. Blades are adjusted to match triangle in gable. Siding and sheathing are then cut out with studs left in place. Screen wire is tacked to siding and studs and vent slips under loosened fascia where it is nailed to siding at edges and into studs.

Shed-hood ventilators are made for hip roofs. Cut made through roof should match rectangular opening in underside of vent. The unit is then nailed to roof sheathing and shingles are nailed over ventilator edges to keep water from going into the attic. Ventilator edges are calked for a watertight seal.

OPENINGS REQUIRED FOR FAN INSTALLATION

FAN SIZE	22″	24″	30″	36″	42″	48″
Full opening (no screen or hardware cloth)	5.5	6	9	12	18	23
Full opening with 16 mesh screen	11	12	18	26	36	46
Full opening with ½″ hardware (cloth)	6.6	7.2	10.8	15.6	21	27
Wood louvers—no screen or cloth	8	9	13.5	19.5	27	34
Wood louvers with ½″ hardware (cloth)	9.6	10.8	16.2	23.4	32	41
Wood louvers with 16 mesh screen	16	18	27	39	54	69
Metal louvers—no screen or cloth	7.2	7.8	11.7	16.9	23	20
Metal louvers with ½″ hardware (cloth)	8.6	9.4	14	20.3	28	36
Metal louvers with 16 mesh screen	14	16	24	33	47	60

Openings are noted in square feet.

■ House with attic—no stairway: a suction box is most effective in this situation since it places the fan further from the intake grille and discharges the hot air in the direction of the roof louvers.

■ House with attic—high gables: place the fan vertically on the outside wall (gable end) to minimize transmission of noise to the rest of the house. This type of wall installation moves the hot air out of a house rapidly.

■ Small house with flat roof: the fan can be installed above the roof line in a small "penthouse" or cupola to protect it from the elements.

The size and placement of exhaust grilles are other important factors to consider when installing an attic fan. Make sure grille openings are protected by louvers or the eaves of the house. Install the vents in the ends of the house away from the prevailing winds.

The exhaust opening is calculated in proportion to the size of the fan. Width and thickness of the louvers and the size and type of the mesh protection should also be considered, since these elements affect the area through which the exhaust air can move. Consult the accompanying chart for correct grille opening.

WALLS AND WALL COVERINGS

What to Use; How to Use It; How to Do It

Man's compulsion to decorate the walls that surround him asserted itself very early in his existence. The remarkable wall paintings that line the Paleolithic caves at Altamira in Spain and Lascaux in France may be as much as 15,000 years old. Rather more recently, the Roman architect Vitruvius, writing a design manual in the first century B.C., offered detailed advice on appropriate wall decorating, adding some grumpy complaints about the decadence of contemporary taste in frescoes.

As indicators of a given historical period, wall decorations are clues as reliable as styles of furniture or clothing. Brilliant tapestries and linenfold paneling typify the Middle Ages as definitely as brocades and gilded plaster do the Renaissance, or as scenic wallpaper and delicate plaster reliefs do the eighteenth century. In modern architecture, the interpenetrating planes of white plaster and clear glass, despite their lack of applied ornamentation, are equally unmistakable as hallmarks of twentieth-century design.

Most of the early wall treatments had a functional as well as an aesthetic purpose: they provided insulation in drafty, damp stone buildings. Perhaps because modern construction methods eliminate this necessity, perhaps because modern design favors stark simplicity, perhaps because a mobile population prefers to decorate its walls with movable prints and paintings—whatever the reason, contemporary wall decoration tends overwhelmingly to plain plaster surfaces painted in a neutral color.

This apparent preference for the bland is certainly not dictated by lack of alternatives. If talented carvers and plasterers are rare nowadays, talented graphics and textile designers are not. An almost limitless variety of prefabricated wall coverings provides a more than adequate substitute for the handcrafted wall decorations of the past. The range of widely available ready-to-use wall coverings encompasses prepasted wallpapers, precut wood paneling, stock molding strips, plastic and ceramic tiles.

The postwar development of plastics has had far-reaching effects on wall coverings. Plastic-based paints, which can be applied smoothly and effortlessly, facilitate do-it-yourself interior decoration. Vinyl coatings render wallpapers, once considered a fragile material, impervious to most stains; and papers so treated are, moreover, completely washable. Vinyl panels simulate the appearance of hardwoods at a fraction of the cost and upkeep of lumber. Lightweight bars of styrofoam imitate ancient oak beams that even an inexperienced carpenter can use to create the appearance of a half-timbered wall.

Choosing your wall covering

Your choice of wall decoration will depend on the role you intend your walls to play in an overall decorating scheme. Because of their extensive area and high visibility, walls constitute a most important decorating element in any room. Certainly you will want to use this major element either to establish your basic

An open bookcase brings out a picturesque wall covering. Shelving, books, and decorative arrangements frame wallpaper views of the exotic creatures and waving foliage of the African veldt. Vertical support is provided by four ceiling-high 3x14s. Drill holes in boards for ¾-inch dowel rods; plate-glass shelves are 12x36.

color scheme or to provide a subtle foil for more dramatic, smaller components.

If you have chosen bold, bright prints for draperies and upholstery, the neutral background of plain painted walls will give them the needed visual space in which to flourish. Similarly, if you want display space for an art collection, you will prefer that walls be unobtrusive and noncompetitive.

A room furnished with handsome antiques, on the other hand, seems to call for a more elaborate and traditional frame in which the furniture can be properly displayed. Exposed timbers and rough plaster, for instance, suit Early American furniture, as painted paneling suits Georgian pieces, or the subtle textures of grass cloth or low-key pure colors suit Oriental- or Indian-inspired furnishings.

A supergraphic can be defined as a wall painting that changes the proportions of its environment. Here are some rules to go by: enlarge everything, explode shapes, juggle colors, look beyond borders. Concealing a door, this supergraphic creates a new formal space that fits perfectly around the sensuously sculptured furniture.

Your style of living, as well as the style of the room's furnishings, will govern the style of wall treatment—whether plaster is rustically rough or urbanely smooth, whether wallpaper is boldly striped or delicately patterned, whether wood paneling is highly polished and trimmed formally with moldings or knotty and laid casually in random widths.

Wall coverings may make a major decorating statement or even provide the entire decoration for a room. A small room occupied only for brief periods can accept an extravagant wall decoration that might prove too strong for, say, a bedroom. A forceful red-and-gold wallpaper, for instance, might overwhelm one's senses in a living room, but would produce a feeling of pleasurable astonishment in a powder room. In an entrance hall, a large mural painted on one wall might provide interest and even a subject for conversation, while in a study it would be an irritating distraction.

Walls and proportion

The size of the room you are decorating will, at least to an extent, limit your choice of wall treatments. As a general rule, use light colors or small-scale patterns in a little room, and use large-scale patterns in a big room. An outsized wallpaper pattern or very dark wood paneling will tend to overpower a small room, while a dainty pattern will appear inconsequential in a more generously proportioned space.

This is, however, only a rule of thumb that can be purposefully disregarded in some cases. Young married couples who have not yet accumulated enough furniture for even a modest flat can "fill" the empty spaces by deliberately overscaling the wall decorations—an arresting op-art mural, for example, or a traditional scenic wallpaper.

Wall treatments can be designed to cure defects of dimension or to camouflage awkward structural necessities like protruding columns. If you feel, for instance, that the ceiling of a room is too high, you can create the illusion of

An unusual color scheme boldly applied to ceiling and walls works with casual furnishings to create a room that is both memorable and comfortable. The use of blue is the key: a low bookshelf matching its background and a luxurious pale carpet are elements that allow the super-graphic treatment to float serenely.

a lower and more sheltering ceiling by artful wall decoration. You might use a wide wallpaper border at the ceiling line, or a paneled dado, or both, to interrupt the vertical sweep of the walls. You might cover the walls with horizontally striped wallpaper, which would simultaneously make the walls seem longer and the ceiling lower. You might paint the walls a pale color and the ceiling a darker shade, or cover the ceiling with a bright, boldly patterned wallpaper in order to lower it visually.

To give the illusion of greater width in a long narrow room, paint the longer walls a light color, the shorter ones a dark color. Such a technique is effective because light colors appear to recede, dark colors to advance. Or you can double the apparent width of the room by facing one of the longer walls with mirrors.

If you want to conceal a protruding column, paint the walls in a darker color than the column to minimize shadow lines. Another technique is to distract the eye from surface irregularities by covering it in an attractive overall pattern or by using highly textured materials.

A traditional dining room takes on impressive elegance when walls are covered with a richly patterned brocade fabric. The painting with its glowing orange tones provides a dramatic accent and adds visual depth.

Plastic-protected foil is a pretty and practical addition to any room. It is as easy to apply as wallpaper; just paste it on or use the self-adhesive variety.

Vinyl-coated fabrics offer a variety of patterns and simulated textures. Scrubbable and scratch-resistant, they do require a special adhesive for application. This simulated-leather treatment comes in 48-inch rolls.

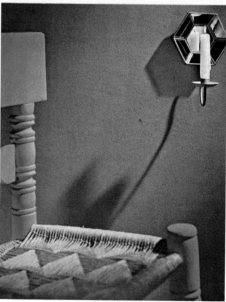

Imagination and scissors are all you need when using self-adhesive waterproof vinyl. Cut to fit; peel off backing; press down and smooth out. This treatment combines two of many patterns: travertine marble and tortoiseshell.

Rugged burlap is a natural for walls in a family room. Besides adding a sweep of color, it can serve as a giant bulletin board. More than a dozen bright colors are available in 18-inch-wide self-adhesive-backed rolls.

Functional considerations

Your selection of wall finishes will also depend in part on the physical punishment they are likely to suffer. The accumulation of moisture in a bathroom, for example, requires that the wall covering be resistant to damage by water. For this reason, ceramic tiles and porcelain enamel are conventional and highly satisfactory choices for bathroom walls.

In the kitchen, where spattering grease and water are inevitable, you will want washable wall surfaces such as tile, glossy enamel, or plastic laminate.

Modern plastics, however, extend your range of choice in wall finishes for those areas where they may be vulnerable to damage of one sort or another. Although real wood would certainly warp on damp bathroom walls, vinyl panels, simulating the appearance of fine wood with accuracy, cannot warp and would lend to any bathroom an air of surpassing luxury.

You can use practical vinyl wallpapers to introduce color and pattern into the kitchen—they are washable, and they will not be damaged by either grease or water. Because they are durable and easily cleaned, vinyl wall coverings are also practical wall finishes for children's rooms. Pliable sheet vinyl and vinyl-coated wallpapers are both available in a wide variety of colors, patterns, and textures.

Wall coverings also perform acoustic (sound-deadening) functions. If you want to reduce the reception of sound in a study, or to minimize the transmission of sound from the children's playroom, line the walls with cork tiles. Carpeted walls are likewise highly sound absorbent,

and present an extremely attractive appearance in a study or bedroom. Fabric wall coverings and flocked wallpapers have less pronounced but still highly effective acoustic properties.

Decorative accents

Walls need not be restricted to the purely passive role of providing background. They can also be utilized to punctuate a decorating scheme, as you might brighten the kitchen with

The texture, color, and acoustical value of wall-to-wall carpet make it an excellent choice for walls. For decorative interest, apply 8-foot-wide carpet to wall with aluminum strips studded with brass upholstery tacks. Walls can also be carpeted in self-adhesive carpet tiles.

Decorate a wall with textured linoleum and add provincial atmosphere to a room. If the wall is papered, remove loose wallpaper to prevent bulging; or apply a surface preparer if necessary. Use a linoleum spreader to cover wall with acoustical-tile adhesive; nail linoleum sheet to wall, guiding on a plumb line. Smooth out sheet from top down and from center out; when covered, nail solid beams in place.

a wall of colorful Delft or majolica tiles. They may serve to unify a decorating scheme, as you might cover one wall of a bedroom with a fabric matching your curtains and bedspread. They may also be used to establish visual organization in a multipurpose room, as you might wallpaper one end of a family room to identify it as a dining area. Or they may be used to furnish entertainment, as you might decorate a child's room with a storybook mural.

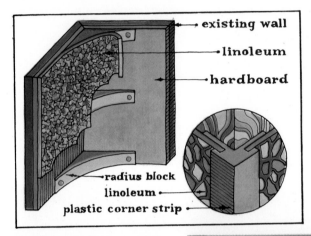

existing wall
linoleum
hardboard

radius block
linoleum
plastic corner strip

Light up a dark basement by using the same bright linoleum on floor and walls. To divide work and play areas, extend a wall pilaster with linoleum-covered box frame; plastic stripping hides seams. Small sketch shows how linoleum fits into plastic strips at corners; covering corners is detailed in separate sketch. Linoleum comes in 12- and 9-foot rolls; cement 12-foot width for flooring, use 9-foot width on walls.

Make a wall come alive by mounting an Oriental rug on fiberboard; use double-face tape at each end to keep fringe in place. For an elegant paneled look, try inexpensive wood-grain hardboard. The grain pattern is reproduced on a vinyl film by means of photographic and lithographic techniques, and the vinyl is then fused to a hardboard base.

By focusing your creative energy on a small special area, you can dare wild color combinations and bold patterns—especially if you use strippable paper. This expression refers to a chemically treated stock that is tough enough to resist tearing while permitting wall covering to release from adhesive. Remove entire strips without wetting.

Natural bark-brown cork brings authoritative texture to a ▶ living room, right. Cork is a relatively easy do-it-yourself project: tiles come with self-adhesive backs; sheets can be applied with acoustical-tile adhesive spread with a trowel. Tissue-thin cork sheets with hand-printed designs are available in rolls 30 inches wide and 15 yards long.

Ready-made aids to special wall treatments are widely available. Ordinary paint, obtainable in a limitless range of ordinary and extraordinary colors, can give you a contrasting wall or alcove quickly and cheaply. Another easy and inexpensive way to enliven plain walls is to trim them with wide wallpaper borders. You may place these borders at the ceiling line, around doors and windows, or to outline permanently placed furniture like a child's study desk or a bedstead.

Better interior decorating shops can often supply matching or coordinating wallpaper and upholstery fabric. If matching wallpaper is unavailable, you can cover the wall with the fabric itself, although this is likely to be more expensive.

Wallpaper

Although historians differ, the Chinese are generally credited with having invented wallpaper, mounting painted rice paper on their walls as early as 200 B.C. Without doubt, Europeans were decorating their walls with printed papers by the sixteenth century.

Advertised as "paper hangings," sometimes called "poor man's tapestry," early wallpaper patterns often simulated the appearance of rich damask wall hangings. Flock papers, composed of chopped wool fibers sprinkled on a patterned ground of varnish or some other adhesive, were particularly valued in the seventeenth century

A garage was turned into a comfortable family room with a rustic atmosphere. The rubblework fireplace was constructed where garage doors previously stood; weathered paneling and beams were salvaged from an old barn.

Random-grooved plastic-finished hardboard paneling gives a new face to a powder room. A refreshing departure from the usual floral backgrounds found in bathrooms, hardboard is convenient for covering cracked plaster, soiled paint, or old wallpaper. Washable paneling comes in 4x8-foot sheets and can easily be applied to the wall with finishing nails slightly countersunk (fill the holes with dabs of paint). Four panels will cover walls of a small room.

Rosewood paneling can transform a neglected wall into one of timeless beauty—the focal point of a room. For a dramatic finishing touch, use doweled battens to secure panels to wall. Place 1½ x ¾-inch battens at 2-foot intervals on 4x8-foot grooved panels and countersink expansion screws on 6-inch centers of battens. Plug holes with ¾-inch dowels, left protruding ¼ inch. Stain dowels.

for their convincing imitation of more costly damasks and cut velvets.

The Frenchman Jean Papillon, working at the end of the seventeenth century, is generally credited with the invention of wallpaper as we recognize it today—a repeated pattern printed so that it can be matched on all sides. During the eighteenth century, both the French—with the encouragement of Madame de Pompadour —and the English developed wallpaper printing as one of the major decorative arts. Their hand-printing technique, sometimes requiring more than a thousand carved wood blocks for a design, produced multicolored papers with great delicacy of line, shading, and color.

The last great historical surge of aesthetic invention in wallpapers resulted in the fashion for scenic papers that emerged in the early nineteenth century. Thereafter the creation of new designs, though not the manufacture, of wallpaper fell off sadly. The invention of the high-speed printing press, the concentration on cost-cutting, and the insensitivity of Victorian taste all influenced wallpaper design for the

◄ A dining area looks on the back of a massive freestanding stone fireplace and its attendant wall. Irregular rows of coursed rubble, a pattern known as ashlar masonry, produce an effect that is natural yet elegant.

Undressed native stone hand-set in concrete makes a subtly colorful fireplace wall and hearth. An old-brick floor carries out the natural theme, contrasting a geometric pattern with the wall's random shapes and pastel tones.

worse. Only the wallpapers of the English arts-and-crafts reformer William Morris relieved this long period of uninspired design—and his papers, although beautiful, were hand-blocked, expensive, and appealed to a limited audience.

While wallpaper has never gone entirely out of use, the garish and dreary patterns that characterized most late-nineteenth- and early-twentieth-century production undoubtedly induced most decorators, until the fairly recent past, to rely instead on plain painted walls.

Postwar developments

The years since the end of World War II have witnessed a steadily growing use of wallpaper.

This interest may originally have been simply a reaction to wartime austerities, and perhaps a rebellion against the bare surfaces esteemed by the Modern Movement. Fashions in home furnishings, from paper towels to major appliances, stressed the use of color—the more unconventional the better.

As with color, so with pattern. The trend for some years has been toward large-scaled, boldly figured design, in wallpapers as well as in textiles and floor coverings. The stylized flowers and brilliant geometrics characteristic of today's wallpapers bear little resemblance to the conservative patterns that dominated the thirties and forties. Even traditional designs, such as damasks, are today apt to be overscaled and executed in surprisingly unconventional colors.

The vinyl revolution
The introduction of plastics into the manufacture of wall coverings has had even more revolutionary effects than the new-found freedom in design. Vinyl is the nearest thing possible to an all-purpose material, and, alone or in combination with other materials, it is the indispensable element in most modern wall coverings. It is washable, proof against tearing or scratching, and resistant to grease, alkali, or water stains.

Patterned vinyl wall coverings are generally made by laminating a layer of clear vinyl over printed paper or fabric. This combination is sometimes bonded to still another layer of fabric backing to add serviceability and ensure a smooth finish. The surface of the vinyl-coated papers may be textured with a grainy or linen-like matte finish or it may be as slick as patent leather for the currently fashionable "wet look".

Heavy-duty sheet vinyl wall coverings are produced chiefly for commercial installations such as in hotel lobbies. At present they are often custom-made, their molded textures are not generally scaled for domestic use, and they

Face brick, brick masonry with ▶ a glazed surface, makes a handsome wall that is completely nonporous and dirt-resistant. Constructed with new bricks, a face-brick wall will never develop chipped corners, and its rich tone will remain.

Old bricks with their unique texture, color, and patina lend qualities of beauty and sturdiness to walls. Setting a brick wall is a relatively easy do-it-yourself job involving patience, a steady hand, trowel, mortar.

Space can be divided with a wall of shoji screens (the Japanese name for translucent wood-framed sliding panels used as room partitioning). These shoji panels slide on a ceiling-mounted track. It is also possible to paper panels with shoji-looking cloth or vinyl of rice-paper texture.

Perforated hardboard is a perennial favorite with youngsters who want to show off their special treasures. It is available by the panel, and the perforations accommodate metal hooks and shelf brackets. The same type of board can be used to handle equipment in kitchen, playroom, or garage.

are quite expensive. Furthermore, these vinyls are manufactured in 54-inch strips, an ungainly width that makes them unsuitable for do-it-yourself installation.

Nonetheless, they are virtually indestructible, and a light-gauge vinyl wall covering may be a worthwhile investment in an area that receives punishing use, such as the kitchen or the children's recreation room.

Olefin, a spun-bonded fabric, is another plastic rapidly gaining favor as a wall covering. Its structure consists of a single filament of olefin plastic randomly laid to cover an area, then treated with heat and pressure to fix its texture. The material has remarkable dimensional stability and toughness.

Foils and flocks

Metal foil wallpapers follow the current decorating vogue for slick, smooth, and shiny surfaces. Gold and silver leaf have been used in the past when interior decorators wanted to create an effect of especial splendor. The application of metal leaf, a sheet of metal no more than five-millionths of an inch thick, is painstaking, however, and labor costs raise the price of an already expensive material still further.

Today, thanks to modern manufacturing techniques, you will not need a princely income in order to afford gold and silver foil wallpapers. A thin sheet of metal—usually gold, silver, or aluminum—is bonded to a sheet of paper to toughen the material and to facilitate hanging.

Patterned foils are also available. They can be overprinted with transparent inks, slightly veiling the gleam of metal, or with opaque inks, producing a highly effective contrast of visual textures. Designs are very often geometric prints, in two or more colors, or luxurious imitations of marble or tortoiseshell.

Flock papers, more or less out of fashion for many years, have regained favor, partly because of recently added practicality. Flocking is now often made of chopped synthetic fibers rather than wool or silk. When this flocking is applied to a vinyl ground, the paper can be washed with soap and water. Flocking is occasionally applied to foil, where the contrast of shiny background and velvety figures furnishes extravagantly dramatic wallpaper patterns.

Patterns

It is difficult to catalog and define wallpaper patterns. For one thing, designers often combine standard motifs, as they might superimpose a floral pattern on a ground of stripes. Nevertheless, it may be helpful to analyze the major categories of patterns in terms of their tradition, their modern adaptations, and the best ways to use them.

■ Damask: a pattern based on the designs for the superlative Italian silks woven during the Renaissance. The major motifs are highly styl-

In a bathroom, all-white walls were covered with colorful strings of beads hung from a ceiling-mounted track. A bead treatment would be an appropriate choice for any short wall whose plainness needs decorative first aid.

Using bamboo on a wall is an easy, inexpensive way of ▶ giving a boy's room an outdoor feeling all year round. Paint the wall a dark color. Stain split-bamboo shade and attach to wall with screws.

ized and symmetrical flowers or fruits, arranged geometrically and enclosed in a network of curving arabesques, also stylized and geometrically arranged. The pattern may have two colors —as a gold figure on a dark red ground—or, in flock papers, only one—as a figure of ivory flocking on a matching ground. The pattern is in all cases a commanding one and is, generally, suitable only to large and formal rooms of special richness.

■ Florals: a catchall phrase that encompasses any wallpaper incorporating flowers, ranging from complex naturalistic designs to overscaled conventionalized motifs only remotely related to flowers. The question of which floral pattern is most appropriate to which decorating style cannot be answered definitively—the choice must be determined by the combination of scale, color, and density employed in the design. As a very rough rule of thumb, however, realistic flowers are suitable to traditional settings, stylized flowers to modern settings.

■ Geometrics: another catchall phrase. Geometric patterns include any overall design based

◄Where there is a view, walls of glass offer beautiful exposure for interior spaces, as in this living and family area. Even without a view, clear acrylic panels, lighted from behind, or shoji also suggest extensions of space.

Achieve a luxurious upholstered look by covering a wall in easy-to-manage suede cloth. Backing of foam rubber provides fullness and tautness; secure with brass tacks.

Add dimension to your walls with trompe l'oeil designs that deceive the eye with uncanny simulations of such decorative materials as cane, wood, brick, leather, grass cloth, stone, and various fabrics. Here, a wallpaper design representing wood-framed cane panels provides classic elegance.

on straight lines, circles, or polygons. They also include those patterns more familiarly called polka dots, stripes, and checks, as well as, in a loose sense, such regular representational designs as lattices, grilles, and tiles. Strict geometrics are commonly associated with modern settings, particularly those wallpapers that are bold in color and scale. The representational patterns do best in eclectic settings. Pale stripes might be an excellent choice for a formal traditional living room, while checks would be cheerful in an Early American family room.

■ Scenic papers: not truly patterns since there is no repeat in the design. Scenic wallpapers,

A dramatic play of light and shadow results from the combination of candlelight and walls of dark cork. Rough-textured cork comes in sheets and large-sized tiles.

usually landscapes but sometimes including figures and buildings, are produced in both traditional and contemporary styles. They are not available in wide variety, however.

■ Textures: not precisely "patterns," textured wall coverings include such genuinely textured materials as grass cloth, a lustrous material woven in the Orient, and shiki, a coarse silk resembling shantung. The appearance of these fabrics, as well as of such materials as marble and tortoiseshell, is often reproduced photographically on wallpapers, and dimensional texture is added, where appropriate, by embossing. Grass cloth and shiki textures are especially becoming backgrounds for Oriental furniture, and all of these textures suit modern decor.

■ Toiles: a design based on the eighteenth-century French *toiles de Jouy* fabrics. Usually a two-tone pattern with delicately rendered drawings in blue, red, or brown on a white or creamy ground, the design repeats pictures of such scenes as nymphs and shepherds frolicking in sylvan landscapes. Or they may consist entirely of stylized floral motifs in monochromatic patterns. These patterns harmonize with eighteenth-century furniture, and are perhaps more at home in a semiformal setting than in an elaborate one.

There are, besides, some familiar patterns that do not fit into any of these categories—exotic paisleys, for instance, or commemorative designs (picture patterns, such as, say, General Washington crossing the Delaware). These tend to be very strong patterns, and a decorator needs a good eye and self-confidence to make proper use of them.

Printing techniques

The cost of any given wallpaper is determined largely by the complexity of its design and the resulting complexity of preparing printing plates, by the number of colors in the design, and by the printing process employed.

The most common process used in wallpaper production is roller printing, in which inks are transferred from a metal roller with raised design blocks to a large printing roller and thence to the paper as it is fed through the press. Roller printing produces most of the low-cost wallpapers, but some expensive papers are also printed by this method.

In the rotogravure process, designs are incised on the printing plate; as the paper moves through the press, it picks up ink deposited in the incision. This process, which uses transparent inks for overprinting, can produce delicate shadings not achievable with roller printing. Some rotogravure wallpapers, utilizing photographic techniques, reproduce convincingly the appearance of such materials as silk fabric or laid brick. To add appropriate texture, the papers are frequently embossed after printing.

The finest wallpapers are produced by the silk-screen process. Essentially a highly sophisticated stenciling technique, the process utilizes large sheets of silk gauze, at least one for each color used in the design. The portion of the design that will not be printed is blocked out by an insoluble coating such as glue or shellac, and ink is squeezed by hand through the uncoated silk screen. Because silk-screening always requires a great deal of handwork—and the more colors in the pattern, the greater the number of hand operations—silk-screened paper is always an expensive product.

Both the rotogravure process and the silk-screen process use oil-based inks, which are washable. Vinyl colors, used in both roller-printed wallpapers and in the silk-screen process, are also washable.

The cost of wallpaper, expectably, varies widely, and you may pay from $1 to $50 a bolt (two rolls, each covering 30 square feet of wall area). The cheapest wallpaper, known to the trade as "skin," is made of paper untreated with any plastic coating, chemical, or ground color, and is printed with unwashable pigments. Obviously, like low-cost linoleum, "skin" is intended only as a temporary covering.

Revive a wall with striped canvas or denim applied with suitable paste. Edge valance with coat binding and staple to a 1x3-inch pine board fastened flat to ceiling.

Installing wallpapers

The techniques for hanging wallpapers, including preparation, cutting, matching, and gluing, are discussed in some detail in the illustrated how-to section below. Special circumstances, however, will require special handling.

Fine wallpapers—antique scenic wallpapers, for example—are customarily mounted on an underlay of muslin to ensure a smooth surface and to protect the paper against cracks. More importantly, the muslin lining facilitates removal so that the paper can be hung elsewhere. The removal of these fine papers is, however, a difficult job that should be entrusted only to a top-notch professional.

Cover a wall with lattice molding. Between two 1x2s, space as many strips of lath as you need and nail them in place. Cut a diagonal strip at top and a circle in the middle. Nail and cement the lath to the wall, but slightly offset the sections. Paint the entire surface in flat white.

Increase the warmth and intimacy of a room with the addition of walnut-stained shakes applied to walls from the bottom up. Imagine the same shingle arrangement made, instead, with mirrors; they are available in gently sloped, slightly faceted individual tiles. ►

It is a good idea to use a paper lining under flock papers and under foils. Both of these wallpapers depend on a smooth surface to display their best qualities, and foil in particular will reflect any irregularities in the surface it covers.

Both flock papers and foils also require special care in installation. Flocking, for instance, has an irritating way of attracting paste. For this reason, the selvage is ordinarily not trimmed until after the strip is on the wall. If paste should spatter on the flocking, it must be sponged off immediately. Further, the seams of flock paper must be smoothed with a soft brush rather than with the usual hard-rubber roller.

If you buy foil wallpaper, be sure to ask the dealer about any limitations on installation. Some foils will tarnish under certain conditions. Both flock papers and foils usually require special adhesives; directions generally accompany the papers and should of course be followed with care.

Do-it-yourself aids

From the view of the do-it-yourself paperhanger, the most welcome improvement in this area must surely be the prepasted wallpapers. Apart from relieving the home handyman of the chore of mixing paste, they eliminate the awkward manhandling of wet pasted strips.

Running a close second to prepasting as a do-it-yourself convenience are the recently developed "strippable" papers. These wall coverings do away with the drudgery of steaming and scraping old paper from walls to be redecorated. They are made of a tough material such as vinyl or olefin that will resist tearing. A special "release" adhesive bonds this covering firmly to the wall until it is pulled away with determination. The stripped walls require no treatment beyond washing to remove any remaining adhesive.

Except for silk-screened wallpapers, most wallpapers now come with selvages pretrimmed, another time-saver for the amateur paperhanger. In some cases the selvages are per-

forated and can be removed either by knocking the end of the roll against the edge of a table or by tearing. Flock papers, from which selvage should not be removed until strips are in place, are often provided with these partially trimmed selvages.

Care and maintenance

Most wallpapers, if printed with insoluble oil-based or vinyl inks, can be cleaned with mild soap and warm water. To make sure your wallpaper is washable, test it in a corner that is ordinarily hidden by furniture.

Under no circumstances should you wash wallpaper with a detergent.

Wash a papered wall in sections, starting at the baseboard and working up. After soaping, rinse the wallpaper with clear water and wipe with a clean cloth. Walls should be washed from the bottom up to prevent stains caused by dripping water; dirty streaks are easily sponged off clean walls, but may—if surface soil is allowed to accumulate for a long period of time—form ineradicable stains.

If your wallpaper is not washable, clean it with a commercially available gum cleaner. This material, which resembles an elastic putty, is used like an eraser to remove surface dirt. Be sure to knead it repeatedly as you use it so that you always work with a clean area. Alternatively, you can clean wallpaper with a cloth dipped in dry borax. There are also products that may be applied to newly hung paper to make it spot-resistant.

Treillage, or latticework wallpaper, is screen-printed to resemble the open-air graces of a gazebo or patio. The pattern establishes the colors of the room and also sets the theme, supported by citrus-fruit colors of upholstery and accents. Screens of rattan also suggest the outdoors.

Grease spots can often be removed with dry-cleaning fluid or with a hot iron and blotting paper. Vinyls are, of course, grease-resistant, but grease spots should be sponged off immediately.

Although vinyl flock papers can be washed, this treatment should not be repeated too often as the flocking will eventually shed. You can clean flock papers safely with a vacuum cleaner and a soft brush. Tough vinyl-coated and vinyl-impregnated wall coverings can be scrubbed fairly energetically but should not be scoured with abrasives.

Patches and other repairs

If wallpaper is torn or deeply scratched, and if you have saved scraps, it is an easy matter to cover the damage with a patch. Tear a piece from the leftover wallpaper, match the edges, and fasten with household glue or wallpaper paste. If you have used prepasted wallpaper, dip the patch in water and fix it in place.

Tearing the edges of the patch is preferable to making straight cuts because the feathered edges will not so readily catch the light and cast shadows. If the wall covering is vinyl or olefin and you cannot tear it, cut the edge in a series of irregular curves.

Should wallpaper work loose at cornice or seams, you can easily repair it by gently pulling enough of the covering away from the wall to apply a dab of white household glue. Press the paper down for a moment or two, then clean off any excess glue with a damp sponge.

Air bubbles that appear after wallpaper paste has dried can also be repaired, although the operation requires a certain deftness. Carefully slit the bubble with a razor blade and insert glue, then press firmly to squeeze out excess glue and sponge off the area. The cut edges will match exactly. However, because not all paste is fast-drying, it may be several days before the paper has dried completely. No such measures should be taken until the drying process is complete.

Wood Paneling

The charm of wood as a wall covering arises from its warm color and beautiful grain, which provide a rich but restrained background for all styles of decoration. Wood offers, in addition, the warmth, texture, and vibrancy of a living material and is thus a valuable complement to materials such as cold glass, stone, or metal.

Plywood panels

Some of the decorative paneling effects known to the past—the exquisite inlays of fifteenth-century Italy, for example, or the superlative carving of seventeenth-century England—are unobtainable at any price in the twentieth century. There are, however, modern substitutes that can take their places without apology in the most elegant interiors. Modern veneered paneling is backed with plywood and is available in all manner of precious and common woods. The stiff, nonwarping character of plywood, a result of its laminated cross-grain construction, eliminates many difficulties of installation and uncertainties of stability.

Because veneers are real wood, they can be finished exactly as you would finish ordinary lumber, with varnish, stain, wax, or paint. Plywoods are available in prefinished sheets as well—that is, panels that have been stained, varnished, or coated with vinyl, and that therefore require no further treatment.

The surface texture of plywood varies widely. For traditional and formal rooms, the most suitable finish is a smooth-sanded surface, perhaps ornamented with moldings. A rough-sawn finish is appropriate in informal rooms or where a definite masculine ambience is wanted. Plywood sheets are often "kerfed"—that is, shallow grooves are cut at regular intervals into the face of the sheet so that a standard 4x8-foot panel resembles planking. In other cases, the surface of the wood is treated with chemicals and scrubbed to remove the softer part of the wood and leave the hard parts in a high relief that emphasizes the grain pattern.

Other paneling materials

As a low-cost substitute for veneered plywood, manufacturers of wall paneling make wood-grain hardboard. The authentic wood-grain pattern is reproduced on a vinyl film by a combination of photographic and modern lithographic print methods, and the vinyl film is then fused to the hardboard base to provide an almost indestructible surface. Besides reducing the cost of "wood" paneling, this process also eliminates unsightly irregularities like knots.

More ingeniously, if more expensively, the same photography-lithography process is used to reproduce wood-grain patterns on a wood veneer. This operation allows a cheaper hardwood such as lauan (Philippine mahogany) to masquerade as more expensive teak or rosewood. Such panels are usually protected by a coat of vinyl.

See also *Plywood,* Vol. 14, p. 2640, and, for how-to information, *Paneling,* Vol. 13, p. 2432.

Wood patterns

The beauty of veneers lies in the particular "figure" each wood possesses—that is, the pattern resulting from the combination of grain, color, and position of annual rings that is individual to each variety.

Logs can be sawn in a number of ways. Plain-sawn lumber, where the cut is made down the entire length of the log, gives a grain characterized by long ovals and steep arches. Quarter-sawn lumber, where the log is first quartered and then cut perpendicular to the center, has a grain pattern of parallel vertical lines. Rotary-cut veneer, where a special knife slices a continuous sheet from the outside of the log, has a complex figure of wavy lines and concentric circles.

Modern manufacturing techniques, as well as photographic processes, have made some

These two pages show attractive examples of modern easy-to-handle wall coverings that are adaptable to any smooth surface. You can apply them quickly, without mess or tedious adjustment, and they can be pulled down from a wall in full strips in a matter of seconds. Most are scrubbable; many are vinyl-coated, prepasted, and pretrimmed. These examples are screen-printed custom designs.

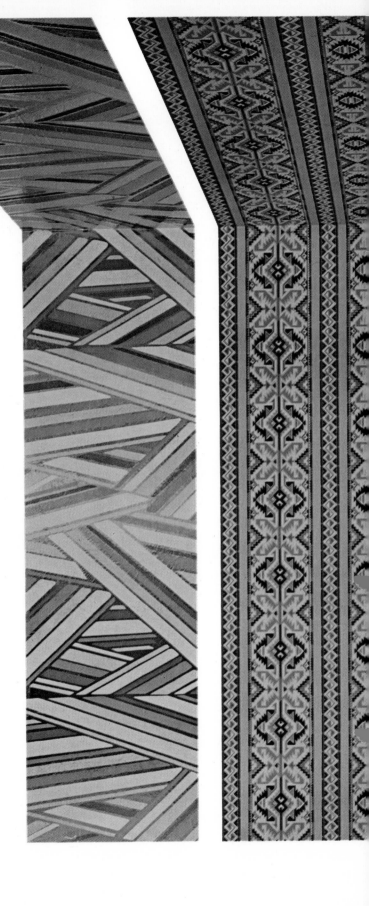

formerly difficult woods amenable to veneering. Ash and elm, for instance, used to be considered too tough and temperamental for easy working, although both of them have agreeable grain and color. Chestnut, Douglas fir, and redwood, which formerly tended to split when worked, have also been tamed by technology.

A choice of woods

Some of the woods used as planks or as veneers or wood-grain patterns in commonly marketed plywood and vinyl paneling include:

Ash: a hardwood, creamy to pale tan in color, with a pronounced and handsome grain.

Birch: a fine-grained blond wood much favored in Scandinavian and other modern interiors; it sometimes shows an undulating "curly" figure.

Cedar: a reddish close-grained softwood; because of its fragrance and its moth-repellent qualities, it is often used to line closets.

Cherry: a highly valued reddish-brown hardwood resembling mahogany.

Chestnut: a grayish wood with a soft texture and a coarse, strongly marked grain.

Cypress: a light brown wood too weak for structural uses but valued for finishing work, especially as "pecky" cypress; it is much used in the south because it is impervious to termites.

Douglas fir: a common softwood varying in color from yellow through red to brown; when rotary-cut, it has a pronounced wavy grain pattern sometimes considered too "busy" for extensive use in interior schemes.

Elm: a porous wood with a delicate and unobtrusive figure, ranging in color from light grayish-brown to dark chocolate.

Hickory: a light-brown, evenly grained wood, difficult to work but now often used as a veneer.

Lauan: a straw-colored or sometimes reddish-brown wood with a distinctive "ribbon" figure; it is often called Philippine mahogany.

Mahogany: the classic hardwood, highly esteemed for its lovely reddish color and beautiful grain; because it is expensive, cheaper woods, such as lauan, are often stained to imitate it.

Maple: a cream-colored to light-brown wood with a straight grain; it is familiar as a standard flooring material.

Oak: a grayish to brown wood with a distinctive open grain and notable durability; American oak is frequently stained to resemble the darker English brown oak.

Pecan: a light- to medium-brown wood with a fairly pronounced grain.

Pine: a common and inexpensive softwood; it varies in grain and color—it may be white, yellow, red, or brown—and is often used for painted paneling.

Redwood: as its name suggests, a distinctly red softwood with a quiet parallel grain.

Rosewood: a hardwood, reddish in color, with broad, curving black streaks; sometimes called jacaranda, it enjoys current vogue as an exotic touch in modern settings.

Teak: a yellow to brown wood with a strong dark grain pattern; it is much used in Scandinavian interiors, where it is finished only with repeated applications of oil.

Walnut: another classic hardwood, light brown to dark chocolate in color, with an unemphatic but handsome grain.

Here is another group of screen-printed wallpapers for easy do-it-yourself application. This type of modern wall covering offers a wide range of exciting patterns and distinctive textures, including wet-look vinyls, sleek foils, and fuzzy flocks. Remove and replace with maximum ease.

All of the veneers discussed above are relatively rare, hence expensive. Because of this consideration, they are used in fine cabinetry.

There are besides some special figures caused by defects in the lumber, or even disease, but these are valued for the beauty or novelty of their appearance:

Knots: as a decorative element, these are seen usually in knotty pine; formerly considered an inferior if not unusable wood, knotty pine was always painted, but the spotty pattern is now popular for informal settings.

Worms: the most familiar example of this diseased wood is perhaps wormy chestnut, where the wood is scarred with irregular holes and tracks left by the attacking worms.

Burls: an excrescence of tiny buds leaves an irregular marblelike figure; a similar defect is the bird's-eye figure unique to maple.

Crotch veneers: these are taken from that part of the log where a branch has forked out, and they bear a V-shaped figure that is often matched in expensive panels to produce a herringbone pattern.

Wood trim

While paneling is a frankly luxurious application of wood as wall decoration, wood as trim is virtually indispensable, whether as baseboards, cornices, or ornamental moldings.

Most lumberyards carry a great variety of shapes and sizes in stock moldings. These may range from the familiar quarter-round molding used as a shoe to finish the joint between baseboard and flooring, through more elaborate denticulated moldings used as trimming beneath Georgian-style mantelpieces, to complexly curved moldings used as ornamental frames for French rococo panels.

To match synthetic paneling, many of these moldings are also available in vinyl-clad wood and in solid vinyl.

For suggestions on decorative applications, see *Moldings,* Vol. 12, p. 2234, as well as *Dadoes,* Vol. 6, p. 1059.

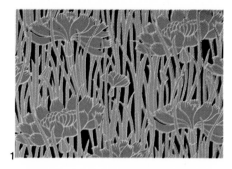

Wall coverings for every room, style, and mood offer limitless decorating possibilities. (1) Elegant stylized flowers form a custom wallpaper design that is available flat or flocked, on paper, vinyl, or specialty stocks. (2) Sugar and spice motif is used on strippable wall covering of spun-bonded olefin-base stock noted for strength and durability. (3) Traditional houndstooth pattern is reproduced on prepasted, scrubbable, strippable, vinyl-coated stock. (4) Field of yellow zinnias decorates strippable wallpaper of olefin. (5) Pattern of stripes

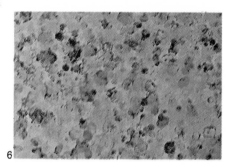

Fabric

Fabrics used as wall coverings offer a softness and variety of texture, a possibility of mixing and matching walls, draperies, and upholstery, and a depth of color not generally available in printed papers. Even an inexpensive fabric covering—say gingham panels in a baby's nursery—provides a feeling of luxury as well as announcing an independence of decorating imagination.

Textiles have been familiar as wall coverings since at least the Middle Ages, when the rich hung tapestries on castle walls and the not-so-rich hung more modest printed woolen or linen panels as decoration. Apart from the aesthetic purpose of adding color and texture to dark stone walls, these hangings served also as thermal insulation. While this function is no longer necessary in modern houses, fabric wall coverings do serve a function as acoustical insulation, especially if the fabric has an underlay of urethane foam.

Any fabric—from $1.29-per-yard denim to the costliest cut velvet or gold-threaded brocade—if properly handled, can be adapted as a wall covering. A rough masculine material like burlap or tweed on walls of a den, a rich silk damask in a formal living room or exotic Thai silk in a modern one, a cheery *toile de Jouy* or

7

8

9

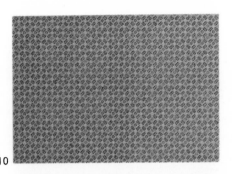

10

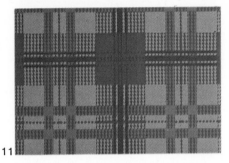

11

12

is pretrimmed and printed in vinyl on wet-strength paper. (6) Shimmering golds and browns blend in a strippable tortoise-shell paper. (7) Glazed mica paper has bold multihued awning stripe. (8) Tiger print is pattern on prepasted strippable vinyl. (9) Mushroom design is printed in grey and white on red vinyl. (10) Small geometric is one of a Colonial portfolio of patterns in correlated papers and coordinated fabrics. (11) Scots tartan in flat psychedelic colors is printed on wet-look red vinyl. (12) Multicolored paisley design is rotogravure-printed on strong smooth paper.

chintz in a bedroom—these ideas serve only to suggest the almost limitless range of opportunities fabrics offer as wall coverings.

A device popular with many interior decorators is to cover the walls of a room with fabric matching the upholstery or the draperies, or both. This treatment helps unify the total decorating scheme.

Modern technology has in this instance also extended both the range of choice and the practicality of fabric wall coverings. The surfaces of many textiles, both natural and such synthetics as the polyesters and acetates, have been treated with chemical finishes to render them dirt-, stain-, and moisture-resistant.

Mounting fabrics

The conventional way to mount a fabric is to stretch it across a light wood frame built to the dimensions of the wall to be covered. The fabric is then secured with upholstery tacks. (An upholsterer, not a paperhanger, is the professional to employ if you do not do the job yourself.) This method is generally the easiest, and it should always be used with fine fabrics like moiré silk or velvet. The panels can then be dismounted for cleaning or for removal to another location.

Less-expensive fabrics, like printed cotton or ticking, can be pasted directly onto the wall. Paste is brushed on the wall or, to ensure a

13

16

14

(13) Pattern of art nouveau flowers, butterflies, and scrolls is available in conventional wallpaper or vinyl. (14) Subtle paisley motif is printed on paper by rotogravure process. (15) Silk-like damask is screen printed. (16) Exotic jungle flowers glow on wet-look vinyl. (17) Scenic wallpaper comes in three panels, plus accompanying background paper. (18) Tulip pattern is available on wet-look vinyl or paper. (19) Geometric,

17

15

18

smooth finish, on a paper underlining. The fabric is then smoothed into place.

Either of these two methods can also be employed for applying relatively small fabric trim on closet doors or for symmetrical panels along a wall. Molding strips will provide a frame for the fabric as well as conceal tacks and raw edges.

If money is no object and your decorating theme is opulence, you can drape gathered fabric with hooks from a rod fixed at cornice height. A similar treatment, equally extravagant, stretches gathered fabric between a rod at the ceiling and another at the baseboard.

See, in addition, *Canvas Panels,* Vol. 4, p. 700.

Paint

The major reason for the continued popularity of paint as a wall covering is undoubtedly its low initial cost. Furthermore, its inexpensiveness makes it expendable, so that you may change your decorating scheme frequently.

Paint also permits a precision in matching colors that is virtually impossible with any other wall covering. With wallpaper, fabrics, or wood paneling, you must take the colors the manufacturers give you. Paint, however, can, with little extra cost, be matched with existing colors or mixed to your color specifications.

19

22

20

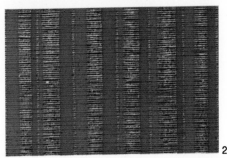

23

angular graphic can be used as wallpaper or framed as art. (20) Silk-screened damask has shadings of metallic gold. (21) Colorful pattern of Napoleonic soldiers is printed on washable fabric-backed vinyl. (22) Brown-and-beige grille pattern with touches of gold is a rotogravure print. (23) Flocking and stripes are combined in stain- and soil-resistant paper with texture of soft velvet. (24) Subtle and subdued damask pattern printed on burlap.

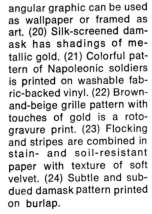

21

24

Additionally, paint is ideally suited to do-it-yourself projects. Its application is easy, especially since the development of latex-based paints that can be applied with felt rollers. Its application is fast, unlike that of, say, wallpaper, which must be carefully cut to measure and matched. And the application of paint presents few pitfalls for the unhandy amateur: equipment is uncomplicated; it requires no dexterity to use; and any blemishes that do appear can simply be repainted.

Which paint to use

In most locations—living and dining rooms and bedrooms—you will want to use a nonreflecting flat-finish paint. These paints are available with either an oil or a latex base. (Latex, incidentally, is a misleading term: although some special-purpose paints do have a rubber base, those commonly termed "latex" paints have in fact a water base with a plastic binder.)

If you are doing the job yourself, you will undoubtedly choose the latex paints. They are easy to apply with either a brush or a roller, and you need not worry about lap marks. They also dry fast enough to allow you to apply two coats, if necessary, in one day. Before they dry, these paints are water-soluble, facilitating the cleanup. (After they have cured, however, latex-based paints are no longer water-soluble.)

On walls that receive great wear or that require frequent washing—the kitchen and the bathroom, possibly the children's playroom—you may prefer a durable, washable enamel. Avant-garde decorators, in addition, currently fancy glossy enameled walls in formal living spaces. Pale or bright enamels reinforce the wet look in modern settings. More daringly, dark enamels—brown, maroon, or blue—are sometimes used in eclectic settings for an unexpected background that is at once sumptuous and rather mysterious.

Glossy enamel is available only with an oil base; oil-based flat and semigloss enamels are also manufactured. Besides these, which are rather difficult to work with, there is a water-based enamel with a semigloss surface.

Alkyd resin paints are also durable and washable, and come in flat, glossy, and semigloss finishes. They are almost completely free of odor and dry very quickly, and they can be applied even over porous materials like masonry without a priming coat.

Casein paints, sold in paste form, must be thinned with water before they are applied. They are inexpensive and easy to apply, and the cleanup can be done with water.

For more detailed information, and for how-to directions, see the article *Paints and Painting*, Vol. 13, p. 2392.

Bold geometric design, supergraphic in scale, turns a wall into a dazzling work of optical art. This scrubbable plastic-coated wallpaper would be a practical kitchen choice.

◄ Achieve a striking modern look by placing three-dimensional stainless-steel tiles on a fireplace wall. Pattern of glowing reflectors is set off by deep-toned walls.

Other Wall Coverings

Despite the traditional use of paint and paper, almost any material can be used as wall covering. Functional necessities sometimes demand a material more durable than paper or paint, and a taste for ostentation may demand a wall covering that forthrightly declares its cost. The materials described briefly here are all frequently used as wall coverings.

Cork

This resilient material is valued for its acoustical properties and because its surface can be punctured repeatedly, as by thumbtacks, without noticeable ill effect. In a study or a library, where quiet is desired, cork provides an efficient sound absorber. In a playroom, a cork wall encourages a changing exhibit of children's art.

Made from the inner bark of the European cork oak, the wall covering is made of small particles of cork held together with a composition binder. Its color is generally a mottled tan and yellow, but tinted cork panels are also manufactured. The material is available in flexible sheets, in square tiles, and in plywood-backed panels.

A fairly recent development in cork wall coverings is the use of large, irregular particles

Doors can be wallpapered, too, if you wish to diminish their importance. This room is unified and made to seem larger by the allover use of a grille-patterned laminated paper that is easily fitted into and around corners.

Floor-to-ceiling wood beams appropriately frame panels ▶ of printed wallpaper inspired by Gothic millefleurs tapestry designs. The dado of wood paneling lends a country feeling, and fireplace wall completes the mood.

of cork fused to a heavy, burlaplike fabric. This fabric may either match or contrast with the cork particles so that, for instance, a bright red burlap may occasionally show between particles of dark brown cork.

Cork's chief disadvantage is its vulnerability to stains, particularly to those caused by grease —a clear vinyl coating provides protection.

Leather

A luxurious wall covering, leather was popular in seventeenth-century Holland, where effects of great splendor were achieved with heavily embossed "Spanish" leather. Treasured examples of this material are still carefully preserved in museum collections.

Today, less expensive vinyl sheets designed to resemble leather are often used where a masculine setting of particular richness is wanted. The surface of this material, like that of real leather, may vary in color and in texture, from suede through soft glove leather to shiny patent leather. Leather-covered walls are often ornamented with molding strips or with brass-headed studs.

Masonry

Most true masonry walls are part of the structure, and they are often revealed as old houses are remodeled. People remodeling city brownstones, for example, frequently find a handsome brick party wall behind an accumulation of paint and plaster; or owners of a renovated stable might decide to leave the inside surface of a stone retaining wall exposed. In most cases, these walls require very little maintenance beyond periodic cleaning and the application of a sealant to protect the porous surface of the masonry against a buildup of soot and dust.

Durable printed foil is used to create a stunning and sophisticated wall treatment. Mellow highlights glitter amid cool sea-green tones and blurred overlapping planes that are reminiscent of classic cubist paintings.

How To Remove Old Wallpaper And Hang New

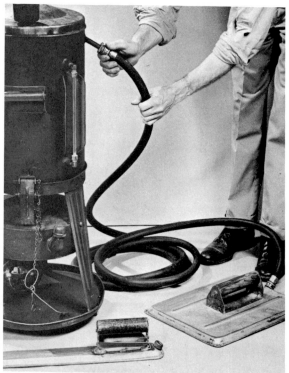

There is just one rapid way to remove old wallpaper—rent a wallpaper steamer from your paint dealer. In a few hours, you will accomplish what would take you days by any other method. Steaming equipment is easy to operate, calling for no special skill or training. It is light, and with reasonable care there is little danger of being burned. The only additional tool you will need is a wide scraper.

Burner and boiler should be kept in ventilated room (not room being steamed) or even outside house so heat will not counteract loosening effect of steam. Wide steam plate is for large wall areas; small one fits tight spots such as those under the windows.

Steam plate has holes in face (against wall) to let steam escape, is light enough to handle with one hand. It is connected to boiler by a long rubber hose. Start removing wallpaper at the lower right-hand corner of a wall (left-hand corner if you are left-handed). Then hold steam plate against an adjacent area with your left hand while you strip loosened paper with your right. Rising steam will loosen paper above area you are stripping.

Ceiling comes last. Rising steam will loosen ceiling wallpaper as you strip walls. Here, ceiling paper loosened and came off by its own weight after a little more steaming. A few trial impressions with the steam plate will show you the most effective length of time to leave in contact. Long sleeves will protect you from warmth of hose.

Doing a room with wallpaper need not be a difficult task. Once you have grasped basic techniques, you can tackle the job with confidence. Photographs in this section show the professional's approach to wallpapering—measuring walls, cutting paper, and matching patterns. Your dealer can figure the number of rolls you will need if you give him dimensions of walls, windows, and doors. Any electrical fixtures and switch plates should be removed before you begin papering. Paper over outlets, then make a cutout around the area. Plate covers ragged edges.

Gather all materials and equipment for papering before you begin work. You can rent most tools, often at store where you select the paper. Tools include: table, steel straightedge, roller knife, seam roller, and smoothing brush. You will also need a sponge, scissors, yardstick, paste, brush, and a string chalk line.

Determine length of the first strip, measuring distance from desired height of paper to baseboard. If walls are freshly plastered or painted, treat with wall "size," water-thin glue applied with brush. At same time, patch any cracks with quick-drying plaster.

Use a plumb line to get first strip straight on wall. It is best to begin in a corner, or at a door or window casing, working to the right. Chalk the line and tack it to the wall near the ceiling or molding about 1 inch less than width of paper. Hold end, snap string for line.

Unroll paper on table for measuring, cutting. Add 8 inches to measurement for trimming at baseboard, ceiling, and for matching pattern. After first strip has been measured, cut with scissors or by "snapping" on yardstick edge.

Unroll next strip. Move it to right edge of first and match pattern or "join" points printed on selvage (arrow). Cut. Stack second strip on top of first, pattern-side up. With drop-match pattern, match every other strip.

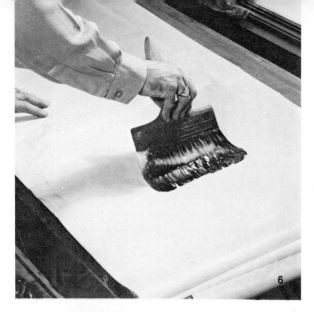

6

9

10

Mix wallpaper paste, adding paste to water, to thickness of beaten cream. Flop stack of strips so first you cut will be first you paste. Apply paste evenly along ⅔ of length; fold strip from its edge to the paste line.

Paste remaining ⅓ of paper to point about 1 inch from end. Fold strip until unpasted end overlaps other cut end. Keep edges even. Do not crease folds; leave slight "roll."

To remove selvage from strip, line up straightedge with the cutoff line. (If there is no distinct line, draw one with yardstick.) Place roller knife, or razor blade, on cutting rule and draw along length of strip.

To hang first strip, hold unpasted end of short fold in one hand and apply at top of wall. Pull out fold with other hand. Be sure right edge follows chalk line; smooth out paper with brush.

Hang second strip, butting edges so pattern matches. Brush air bubbles out from center of strip to edges. To trim paper, crease at baseboard and ceiling with back edge of scissors. Cut on crease. Paste and hang next strips in order you cut.

8

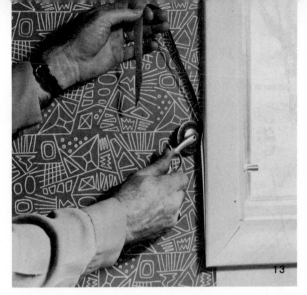

To assure tight butt joints, edge of strips should be rolled with seam roller (or furniture caster). Begin at top where edges touch and roll toward the floor. If the paper gaps, you can usually slip it with your free hand to cover any noticeable error in joining.

Next to door or window, measure from strip to casing; take widest reading and add 1 inch for overlap. Split strip to desired length. Save balance for piecing; do same in corners where paper continues on adjacent wall. Balance of strip will overlap the corner strip.

Press edge of strip into casing. Brush from center to edges to work out wrinkles. With scissors, cut slit at top and bottom where paper overlaps. Wheel-trimmer gets in close to cut off excess. When you begin hanging paper next to doors and windows, trim it this way.

Piece out around doors and windows with strip you split to left of casing. If wallpaper is waterfast (washable), go over entire surface with sponge dipped in clear water to remove excess paste. Sponge each strip as it is hung. If paper is not washable, wipe with clean cloth.

Last strip you hang overlaps left edge of first strip applied. Do not butt edges. Edge of strip at right turns corner to take care of wall that could be out of plumb. Match pattern closely. With ½-inch overlap on right edge, you will have plenty of excess to slip paper.

Prepasted Paper: Wet It and Hang It Up

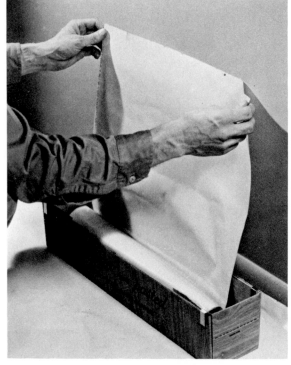

To hang prepasted pretrimmed paper, measure and cut strips the same way as unpasted paper. When all strips in roll have been cut and stacked, reroll strips in order you cut them, pattern side in. Rolls should be loose enough to soak thoroughly. You can get pasteboard water tank from the dealer who sells you the prepasted wallpaper.

Fill tank with water to dotted line. Move tank to spot just below where you will hang first strip. Submerge rolled strip. Weight it with knife or metal rod.

When paper is well saturated, withdraw from tank, holding it at edges. Work from a stepladder or steady chair to bring the paper to molding or ceiling. Press top of the strip onto the wall. Leave excess for matching pattern, trimming. Then work down the wall, taking care to smooth the paper as you go. Move the tank and hang the other wallpaper strips in identical manner.

There is no larger area of color in your room than the four ▶ walls and ceiling, or fifth wall. This mass of color sets the stage for your furnishings; by your choice of treatment, you can create a subtle background or a bold focal point. Elegant flocked wallpaper and matching green velvet draperies add a rich textured look to this living area. Tasseled valance at corner windows unifies scheme and keeps it from being divided by expanse of glass.

In some modern interiors, walls are faced with thin panels of marble, travertine, or slate. These materials are, of course, quite heavy and thus require special anchoring. Since they are expensive materials to start with, the special construction techniques and the necessary labor costs make them very expensive wall coverings indeed. Also, they may be completely out of the question if the basic structure of the house is not adequate to support the added weight.

Less expensively, stone and brick walls are simulated with molded polyester sheets. This relatively lightweight wall covering reproduces the texture of, say, a brick wall both in its larger scale, as tooled joints, and in its smaller

Carpet gives pep and protection to a boy's room. Such a wainscot is easily duplicated when you apply the carpet with mastic. Trim top edge of wainscoting with molding.

The beauty of paint is that it gives you the opportunity to mix colors of your choice. Here, walls have been painted to match curry-colored vinyl flooring. With a large wall area to be covered, and an abundance of light coming from the window wall, a dull or semigloss paint is preferable to a more reflective high-gloss surface.

Stock Williamsburg molding applied to white plaster walls gives a living room a handsome traditional look. Authentic old plaster walls consisted of a coating applied to rough stonework. To duplicate this effect, mix and float with water and, in some cases, with oil; apply with either trowel or brush. Glaze when dry for antique look.

scale, as chipped edges. These sheets are a popular do-it-yourself material; installation requires simply that the material be nailed directly to studs, the nail holes filled in and then concealed with a matching paint.

Mirrors

Glittery mirror walls are a major component of the supershiny interiors currently so fashionable. Besides providing a sparkle of their own, mirrors reflect the dazzle of the bright metals and sharp spotlights that are also inseparable components of this style.

The use of mirror as wall covering is by no means confined to modern decoration, however. Traditional decoration makes frequent use of the pier glass, a ceiling-high panel of mirror framed with stained or gilded molding. In elegant eclectic rooms, the chimney breast or even an entire wall is often paneled with mottled smoked mirror for a rich and unusual effect.

A major function of mirrors in interior decorating is, of course, to produce illusion. A single mirrored wall can double the apparent size of a small room. Facing mirrors carry space out to infinity. Less grandiosely, a projecting col-

Pecky cypress, a handsome, inexpensive light-brown wood, ▶ provides an effective backdrop for a show of American Indian rugs. Cypress is also used as ceiling treatment; cased beams are constructed by mitering three boards to resemble solid beams without their weight and cost.

◀ (Preceding page.) Total-environment jungle scene is a boy's-room entertainment. Walls and cabinet are hand-painted in a manner adapting the styles of popular children's author Maurice Sendak and French primitive Henri Rousseau. For the amateur painter, dealers offer stencils of varied and imaginative designs packaged in kits.

Paneling of butternut (also called white walnut) enhances an eclectic room scheme. It is a wood that works well with practically all colors and styles of furnishings. Paneling is available in widths up to 24 inches and in lengths to 12 feet. After installation, paneling is improved by one or more coats of alkyd varnish and a final application of quick-drying hard-paste wax for protection.

Living area is modernized by a sophisticated background of brown and white. Two walls are covered in a contemporary trellis-design wallpaper whose panels are interspersed with windows concealed by narrow-slat blinds. Mylar bands provide backdrop for Oriental sculpture.

Mellow blending of woods establishes the restful mood of ▶ this room. Wall paneling is prefinished teak, the light tones serving as a foil for art collection. The walnut chairs and the rosewood base of the coffee table add a dark, richly grained hue and also serve to unify scheme.

◀ Decorative possibilities with modern materials are almost endless. Here, beams and walls are covered in vinyl sheeting; one wall is accented by green vinyl. Draperies and pillow slips are of rayon; carpeting is sculptured nylon. Everything is protected with a silicone finish.

To set the base of a living-room "L" apart from the main section of the room, give it character all its own. Cover the walls with paper-backed burlap or felt. Then apply 2-inch prepainted molding strips horizontally, and counter with perpendicular strips at 4-foot intervals. You can get a more traditional effect with braid.

umn in a city apartment might be faced with mirrors simply to provide distraction from its clumsy shape.

Mirrors are relatively expensive to install, costing, at a very rough estimate, about three times as much as medium-priced wallpaper. In compensation, however, the material is for all practical purposes permanent; the threat of casual breakage is quite slight if the mirrors have been properly framed and braced—a job best left to the professional.

For further information, see *Mirrors,* Vol. 12, p. 2182.

Murals

Wall pictures, the oldest known interior decoration, remain a favorite way to give a room individuality. They can be sublime, like the great Italian baroque murals, or simply endear-

ing, like the fanciful mural for a child's room that illustrates this article.

Murals enjoy the favor of avant-garde decorators, too. The so-called "supergraphics," broad swaths of color curving boldly across the flat and cutting heedlessly across corners, have a forceful and exciting presence, although other decorations must be restrained if the total effect is not to appear excessive. Op-art and pop-art designs also lend themselves to modern wall decorations.

A mural, properly speaking, is necessarily a specially commissioned work of art. For non-artists and people with no artists among their acquaintance, however, traditional scenic wallpapers and contemporary pictorial wall coverings of vinyl are commercially available.

At a considerably more modest level, newlyweds decorating their first apartment may con-

A framed work of "art" is actually made of several hundred 2-inch squares of mirror tile. Tiles are not all glued flat; by using varying amounts of adhesive and pressure, many corners and sides were left tilted so they project slightly and catch the light. Backing is plywood.

Glossy patent-leather look can be achieved with many ▶ materials, ranging from genuine leather to vinyl. In fabric, patent-leather looks are less durable, although more adaptable and tactile. Here, a smooth stark surface emphasizes the visual excitement of a bright construction painting.

Richly textured cork wall reaches from oak dado to sloping beamed ceiling in a cheerful living room. An eclectic mix of shapes and textures includes vinyl flooring, shag area rug, and large-scale upholstery and drapery print.

Printed velveteen in a reversible damask pattern appears ▶ in the bedspread and in the shade cloth covering a window behind the headboard. Rich walnut-finish woodwork provides depth and contrast.

Stone and wood are natural partners, especially when they are related by textured carpeting and upholstery. A massive stone-and-cement fireplace wall is combined with walls of prefinished elm paneling for cool outdoor feeling.

◄Dining area takes on a look of provincial elegance and solidity with combination of limestone walls, dark beams, and timber pattern. Walls are of random ashlar masonry construction, consisting of rows of irregular blocks.

sider the poster as a mural substitute. In what amounts to a minor decorating revolution, colorful posters, in all sorts of antique and modern designs, are obtainable in sizes ranging from large to enormous. Costing very little, these disposable murals allow you to experiment to your heart's content. See *Murals*, Vol. 12, p. 2250.

Tile

Its imperviousness to moisture and its washability make ceramic tile a customary choice for bathroom walls. Despite its relatively high initial cost, it may prove a long-range bargain if family members habitually take long, hot showers that would shorten the life of a less durable material.

The only maintenance required for ceramic tile is the occasional recalking of the wall joints around the bathtub—and with the development of plastic calking compound, the necessity for this repair has been much reduced.

Bathroom wall tiles are also available in solid vinyl and in porcelain enamel (a metal tile with a vitreous surface). All of these materials come in a range of colors, and all are suitable for installation by a reasonably deft and patient do-it-yourselfer.

Ornamental tiles, used as a fireplace surround, perhaps, or as a kitchen-counter backsplash, add an air of special distinction to any interior. Traditional patterns include Delft-type scenes, usually produced in blue or sepia and white, and multicolored majolica tiles, based on the geometrical designs of the Spanish *azulejos*. Your dealer may not carry these tiles in stock, but most decorating stores can provide catalogs and will order them for you.

For information on installing tiles, see the article *Tiling,* p. 3082.

Cover plain stucco walls, plus ceiling, with a colorful printed fabric, leaving one wall exposed for textural interest. You can easily do the job yourself with double-faced tape, a staple gun, and fabric adhesive, or use a fabric with self-adhesive backing.

◄ Used in quantity, natural materials have a beauty and integrity that few man-made things can equal. Here, a magnificently proportioned fireplace wall of fieldstone soars from floor to ceiling, creating a natural focal point. Slit windows at either side accent the wall and an airy wall of windows balances and opens up the room, keeping the stone from dominating. The smooth, honey-colored wood paneling that covers the ceiling and wall is a natural complement to the rugged stone.

A sensuous, subtly colored, elegantly executed Persian miniature, magically transformed into wallpaper, provides the decorating keynote for this master bedroom. The rose-petal pink in the wallpaper is repeated throughout the room—in the bedspread, the upholstery, even around the rims of the lampshades. The architectural shapes found in the wallpaper are used in the furniture—domes, turrets, doorways, and lacy screens are echoed by the finials of the bed, the openings of the bookcase, and the supports of the desk, shown at right. Other Oriental touches—the bamboo chair, the Chinese-style bedside tables, the figure of a Buddhist monk supporting the lamp, the Sinhalese bronzes displayed in the bookcase—all contribute to a feeling of exotic luxury. The white rug and furniture give an impression of serenity and space that harmonizes well with the dreamlike quality of the wallpaper.

How to Remove and Build Walls

Remove only nonload-bearing walls

If tearing out a wall is part of your remodeling project, you will first have to determine whether the wall is load-bearing or nonload-bearing. A load-bearing wall is simply

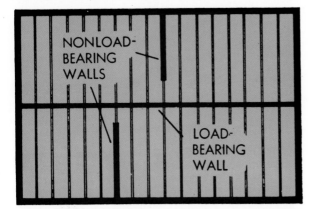

a wall that helps to support some part of the house structure above it. Nonload-bearing walls just partition off space and can be removed without affecting the house structure. You can tell if a wall is load-bearing or not by going up to your attic and noting which way the ceiling joists run in relation to the wall. If the joists run parallel to the wall, and if there are no struts or braces from the roof bearing on top of the wall, the wall is nonload-bearing. Walls that run at right angles to the joists are load-bearing. If the ceiling joists are not visible, you can usually count on the fact that load-bearing walls run parallel to the longest dimension of the house. Should it become necessary to remove a load-bearing wall, a beam to support the weight of the structure above must be used to replace the wall. This beam spans the length of the wall section removed and rests on the adjoining walls of the house, which then bear

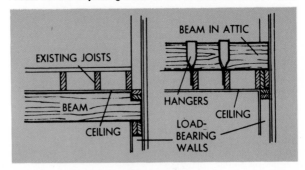

the load. The easiest way to do this is to lay the beam across the ceiling joists in the attic. The ends rest on the plates at the top of the walls running at right angles to the wall being removed. The joists are then fastened to the beam with metal hangers before the wall comes out. If you have a finished attic and cannot run the beam across the top of the ceiling joists, it can go under the joists, projecting down into the room. The ends of the beam are again supported by the adjoining walls. Additional studding must be installed between the studs in the supporting walls for the beam to rest on. Taking out a wall is a messy business, especially if the wall is covered with plaster. Be sure to protect the floor with a tarpaulin before you start. Examine the wall to determine whether any electrical or plumbing lines run through it. A trip to the attic and the basement will give you this information. Arrange ahead of time for professional help to reroute these lines when they are exposed. Begin taking out the wall by removing base shoe, baseboard, ceiling molding, and wall covering. Remove the studs by cutting each one at a slight angle near the bottom. Then remove the sill plate from the floor and top plate from the ceiling. When floor, ceiling, and walls are patched, job is finished.

Framing for new walls goes in easily

Putting in a wall is often considerably easier than taking one out. It is mostly a matter of careful workmanship

coupled with a minimum knowledge of carpentry. Begin by laying out the position of the new wall on both the floor and the ceiling. You then build a studding section to fit the space. Unless the wall is over 12 feet long, assemble the sections flat on a level floor. The studding sections are merely a series of 2x4 studs with 2x4 plates nailed along the top and bottom. Space studs 16 inches on center, or vary them as necessary to fit the covering material used. Double frame around doors and install 2x4 headers over openings. Raise the wall and position it

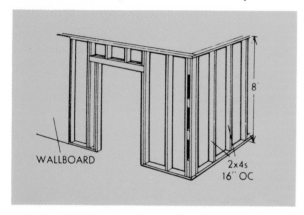

carefully, checking to make sure it is plumb. Use small wood wedges between the top plate and the ceiling to secure the sections temporarily while you nail them in place. If your new wall runs at right angles to ceiling joists, just nail ceiling plate to joists. If the wall is parallel to the ceiling joists, and between them, cut some short lengths of 2x4 and install them between the joists from the attic side. Fasten the top plate of the wall to these nailers. Nail floor plate to floor joists and frame in corners to provide a nailing surface. Cut out floor plate for door openings after wall is in place.

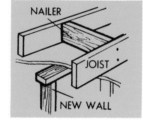

Paneling of wallboard installs quickly

Wallboard is easy and inexpensive to use for covering the rough framing of your new wall. You can cut it to size with a knife, and minor errors in application are easily covered with spackling compound before painting. You simply nail the wallboard in place over the studding, dimpling each nailhead below the surface with last hammer blow. Fill all joints and blemishes with spackle. Press joint paper into flat joints and inside corners with a broad knife. Finish outside corners with metal corner strips; smooth with spackle. Paneling comes in a variety of materials, prices, and textures. All of it has low-maintenance characteristics, however, which makes it a good covering for walls in high-traffic areas such as family rooms, living rooms, and kitchens. In general, paneling is simply nailed over the studding with small finishing nails, or glued in place to avoid showing nailheads. Some types use installation clips.

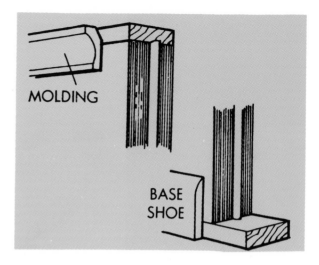

"Sandwich" panels speed construction

One new type of wall material is formed from two sheets of gypsum wallboard with spirals of wood sandwiched between them. These wood spirals give the wall great strength while contributing little to its weight. Wiring and plumbing lines can be pushed through the spirals. The panels rest on floor fittings, as shown in the illustration, and are nailed to a ceiling track. Short lengths of 2x4s, driven into edges of the panels, make the joints. Joints and corners are finished with spackling compound and joint paper—just as with any other wallboard. Another new prefabricated wall section comes completely finished in several choices of simulated wood-grain patterns. The wall sections rest on wood battens nailed to the floor to establish the position of the new wall. They are held in place with moldings nailed to ceiling and floor. The panels have tongue-and-groove edges for easy and rigid joining. A special advantage of this system is that you can also buy matching panels to finish other walls of the room you are remodeling. Just nail 1x2 furring strips to the other walls, then install the panels over them with a staple gun.

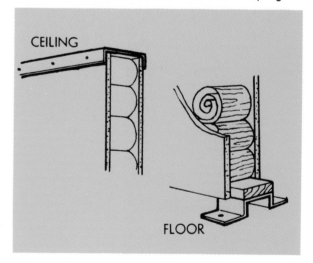

A Look at an Area of the Home Usually Overlooked

Naturally occurring hot water is not unheard of. Its presence, in widely scattered reservoirs around the country, negates to some degree—Fahrenheit or otherwise—the uncomfortable connotation implicit in the age-old expression about "being in hot water."

Only a comparative handful of homeowners are able to pick residential sites above such fortunate locations. That means that for the majority, household water supplies—for bathing, dishwashing, laundering, and so forth—must be heated at some point along the pipeline before reaching the faucets marked "Hot."

Water heaters

This calls for a heating unit, fueled with either oil or gas, or powered by electricity. Water heaters call for careful consideration on the part of the homeowner. They come in assorted sizes, offer varying recovery rates—the time re-

Pure water, in nature, is a rarity. Rainfall, by the time it reaches earth, picks up dust, smoke, living organisms, and gases. The earth serves as a sieve, removing living organisms and turbidity from surface water as it seeps into the ground. But this water, tapped by many households, contains concentrations of dissolved minerals, chiefly calcium and magnesium. These minerals contribute to water hardness. Hard water is found in 85 percent of the U.S.

WATER HARDNESS MAP

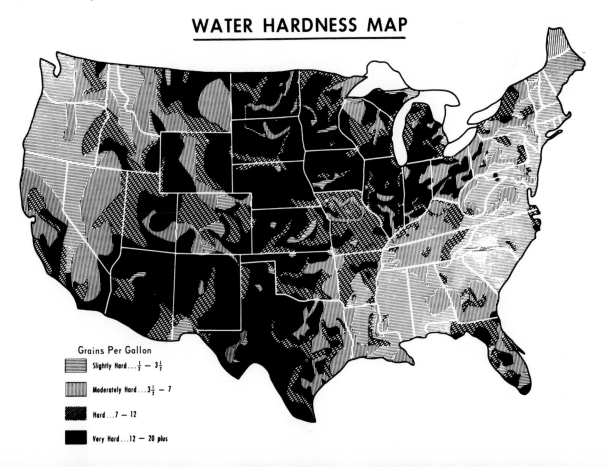

Grains Per Gallon

Slightly Hard... $\frac{1}{2}$ — $3\frac{1}{2}$

Moderately Hard... $3\frac{1}{2}$ — 7

Hard... 7 — 12

Very Hard... 12 — 20 plus

quired to replenish the hot water supply that has been used—and differ considerably in cost.

Before making a choice, determine as carefully as possible your household hot water requirements. There are, for example, some rough hot water consumption measures that can guide the homeowner in making his selection. These include:

- Meal preparation .... 3 gallons per meal
- Dishwashing, by hand .... 3 gallons
- Automatic dishwasher, one load 7-10 gallons
- Tub bath .... 12-15 gallons
- Shower bath .... 10-15 gallons
- Conventional washer, one load 17½ gallons
- Automatic washer, one load .. 15-30 gallons

Remember these measurements are for individual operations. Such hot water demands arise throughout the day but may well overlap during peak periods such as the morning off-to-work and off-to-school rush when faucets marked "Hot" are open and water is in use in bathrooms, kitchen, and utility room.

Once your hot water needs are determined, a reliable plumbing contractor can guide you in the selection of a water heater that will meet all requirements.

Size is not the only critical factor. A 50-gallon heater with a good recovery rate, normally calculated as the number of gallons that can be heated 100 degrees in one hour, may well outperform a heater with a larger capacity—perhaps 80 or 100 gallons—but with a slower recovery rate.

Automatic controls are available on a number of water heaters, with timing devices that provide for an increase in the water temperature during peak demand periods. Temperature controls permit a range of settings, including "normal" for regular use and "low" for a vacation.

Quality water heaters, with a service life of ten to fifteen years, generally carry manufacturers' guarantees that cover leakage and other problems. Check the fine print on the guarantee carefully, as with any appliance, to make sure precisely what is covered and for how long.

Beyond the heating elements, which wear out with constant use, the major internal problem for water heaters is corrosion. Chemicals naturally occurring in water eat away at galvanized steel or copper tanks and eventually cause leaks.

To combat corrosion, water heater manufacturers provide, among other things, porcelainized enamel lining as well as a magnesium rod to attract the chemicals in the water. Lin-

Untreated and ignored, hard water—particularly when ▶ heated—can cause corrosion and scaling. The scaling, unseen but occurring continually inside pipes, valves, water heaters, and outlets, eventually chokes off water flow and reduces the operating efficiency of water heaters. This adds to the cost of obtaining hot water.

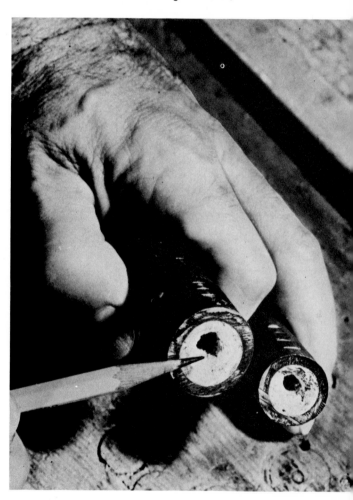

ing and magnesium rods help, but water heater life may be prolonged with regular maintenance efforts. At least once a month draw off a small quantity of water. Drain heaters completely every three to six months; this helps remove mineral deposits and sediment. Check units regularly for signs of leaks. Prompt and regular attention to these details can keep homeowners who have selected fully adequate, quality water heaters constantly in—not out of—hot water.

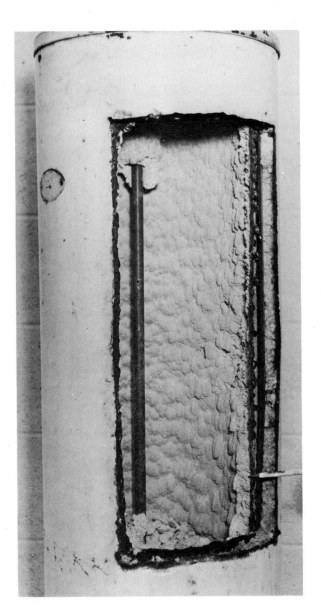

Water softeners

The corrosion that takes place inside water heaters is an invisible manifestation of a problem shared by most homeowners. The problem is hard water.

Visible manifestations of water hardness, which occurs in significant amounts throughout much of the United States, include rings in the bathtub that resist normal scrubbing efforts, cloudy stains that appear on thoroughly washed glassware, scaling that shows up in metal pots, and soap that will not produce suds.

Visible or invisible, water hardness and the problems it causes in residential water systems are genuine and treatable. Homeowners who ignore such matters face not only less than fully efficient operation of water heaters and other water-using appliances but eventual costly repairs on plumbing and pipeline systems throughout the house.

Water hardness is caused for the most part by minerals—primarily calcium and magnesium—dissolved from the earth's crust. It is measured in "grains." Before buying or building a home you should check with the local water department, water company, or a water engineer. They can report on the number of grains per gallon that are found in the local water. If the report is one to four grains, the water is soft and acceptable for almost any use. A report of four to seven grains indicates medium-hard water and ten grains or more indicates very hard water.

A water softener is desirable in areas where the water is medium hard and clearly indicated in areas of very hard water. When hard water is heated, the minerals it contains are reconverted into insoluble limestone, which forms scale deposits in pipes, valves, dishwasher jets, shower heads, and so forth. Water flow is impeded and, inside water heaters, the scale serves as an insulator, decreasing efficiency and increasing fuel bills. A water softener prevents the formation of damaging scale and will also slowly remove previously formed scale.

Water softeners range from packaged products that may simply be added to laundry or dishwater for each individual use to units of varying size and cost that are, once installed, an integral part of a household's water system. The packaged products, including those containing phosphates and marketed under assorted "whiteness" banners, have encountered strong opposition in some areas because they pollute streams and rivers. In certain sections their use has been prohibited.

Regardless of their size, water softening units all basically work on the same principle. They contain a special resin bed. Incoming water passes through this bed, which attracts and holds the calcium and magnesium. Softened water results and is then passed on out of the unit and into the pipelines. A typical installation arrangement for maximum benefit places the water softening unit at a point where the water main enters the house. The water softening unit is then connected directly to the water heater.

The resin bed of the water softener builds up calcium and magnesium deposits and requires regeneration via a backwashing or rinsing with a brine solution. The brine solution is then drained from the unit and the resin bed is ready for continued use.

Nonautomatic, manual, water softening units call for each of the regeneration steps to be started and stopped by hand. Other units are equipped with semiautomatic or fully automatic controls that initiate the cycle at any interval.

Water softening units can be bought or rented. Rates and effectiveness vary and homeowners should check carefully with reputable dealers before making their choice. A fully automatic unit costs about $500.

As in the case of water heaters, the size of the water softening unit depends on the water usage of a household and the degree of hardness in the water. A rough rule of thumb to follow: figure on about 50 gallons a day for each member of the household.

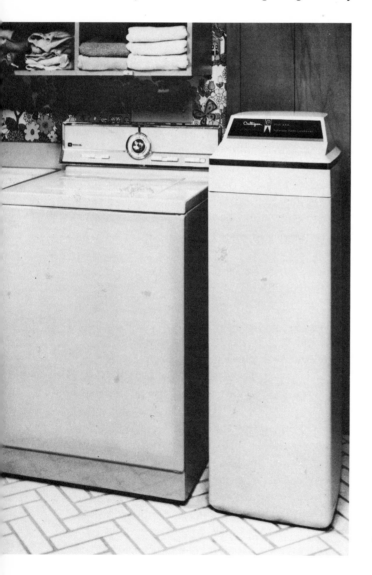

Fully automatic water softening units permit regeneration or backwashing to be done at predetermined intervals. Electrical controls operate valve mechanisms and a clock times each step and returns the entire unit to service. A separate salt-dissolving container is included to provide a supply of salt for a number of regeneration cycles. Newest units feature an electronic sensing device that initiates regeneration automatically. It acts as a hardness thermostat, keeping track of variations in water demands and the varying degrees of water hardness. Fully automated water conditioners, in compact cabinets, are now available for residential use. One type, shown at left, is set alongside a normal clothes washer to indicate its size, although it would not logically be placed in the laundry center. Units such as this remove major impurities from household water, including iron and hydrogen sulfide.

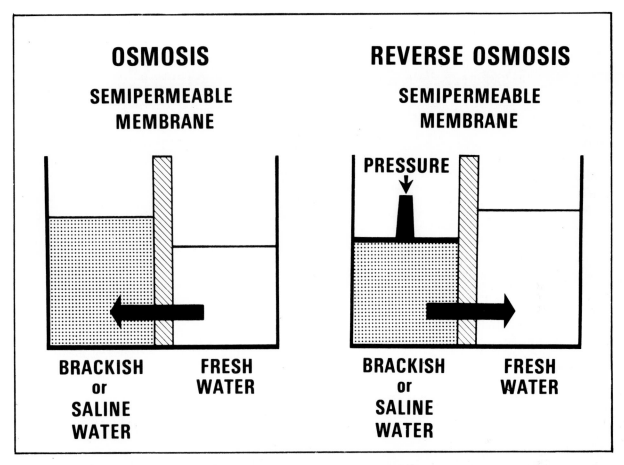

OSMOSIS

SEMIPERMEABLE MEMBRANE

BRACKISH
or
SALINE
WATER

FRESH
WATER

REVERSE OSMOSIS

SEMIPERMEABLE MEMBRANE

PRESSURE

BRACKISH
or
SALINE
WATER

FRESH
WATER

Osmosis is the process whereby plants acquire water and nutrients from the ground and lift these solutions throughout their structures. Osmotic pressure is developed when a less concentrated solution moves through a membrane to a more concentrated solution. Reverse osmosis works in the opposite direction. Artificial pressure is applied to the more concentrated fluid to force water through a special membrane permeable to water but not water impurities. The result is separation of water from its impurities and the providing of soft water.

Water engineers and water heater manufacturers, continuing their research and development work on water hardness and impurities, have recently made available units that encompass a wide range of water treatment by a process known as reverse osmosis. This technique for water purification revolves around a very thin plastic film or membrane that has no pore openings. The membrane removes bacteria and other living organisms and nondissolved solid materials as well as virtually all of the dissolved minerals in the water. Under sufficient pressure the purified water passes through by diffusing into and through the membrane structure. Only three things are involved: water to be treated, the membrane, and water pressure.

Reverse osmosis units are obtainable with capacities of 20 to 500 gallons per day. There are also home-size units that may be installed on or below standard kitchen wall cabinets or on any wall where a water line is available. These latter give 3 to 5 gallons per day of high-quality water for home drinking and cooking needs. Reverse osmosis units, regardless of size, require no regeneration and remove 90 to 95 percent of dissolved solids from water.

Old-Fashioned or Oriental?
No—Always in Style

Forty years ago, wicker was used only for porch furniture. Today you can use it in any room in the house. Cheerful, lightweight, easy to maintain, it blends with almost any style of furniture except in the most formal rooms.

Wicker is a generic name for any furniture made of woven reeds. Rattan is a specific reed that comes from Indonesia and the Philippines. It is a member of the palm family, and can grow to be several hundred feet high. Unlike bamboo, which is hollow, rattan is a solid wood. The core is used in furniture for structural support, while the peel is used to lash the supporting elements together.

Unfinished rattan has a pleasant tan-ivory appearance, although it can be painted and repainted to fit in with any decor. You can achieve

Indoors or out, this chair and table combination would brighten any setting. The functional open-sided forms provide storage space for books, magazines, or pillows. A sturdy steel frame supports the chair. Rattan creates textural interest in a room and can be used either to contrast with glass and tile or complement wood surfaces.

Everything about this family room is comfortable and cozy. The plump, soft shapes of the wicker chairs, the fur-covered hassocks, the pile of pillows, and the short, broad candles accent a room that was designed for casual living. A wicker basket holds an informal arrangement of zinnias whose cheerful colors complement the brightly striped fabric on the chairs.

Evoking soft summer twilights and drowsy afternoons, this ▶ ensemble of ornate wicker furniture, woven in an old-fashioned style, has great charm and utility, and will probably outlast many summers of use. Here it turns a backyard into a spot for gracious living, but it would fit equally well into many areas indoors. Wicker furniture like this is now available in fourteen different finishes including white and natural rattan.

a striking effect by furnishing a room with white rattan cushioned with brightly patterned fabric.

Wide variety of designs

Rattan furniture has been used in the Orient for centuries; it has, however, become commercially available in the United States only in the last fifty years. Much of it is still made in Hong Kong in small family-owned shops. Other rattan furniture comes from China and Spain.

Designs range from whimsical reproductions of Victorian motifs to modern. Many patterns suggest the style of the British colonial empire. A high-backed enclosed chair that may

Versatile cubes of unfinished rattan have a multiplicity of possible uses. Here, they serve as low tables, holding dessert and coffee. They might also function as background for groupings of art objects, as hassocks, as end tables, or as stands for flower arrangements.

A wicker chaise lounge from the Victorian era gets a new lease on life in this comfortably eclectic corner. A distinctive piece like this one would be a charming addition to a garden room or feminine bedroom or dressing room and could always double as elegant patio furniture.

Breaking from the traditional concept of wicker, the bar unit has been constructed along more sophisticated lines. It is ideal for a small room where a solid wood bar would be overpowering. Vinyl seat covers and a Formica bar top resist spills and wear well.

appear in a decorator's catalog as a "hooded cabana chair" would be familiar to an Anglo-Indian as a distant relative of the howdah that is used for riding on elephants. Other offerings of the wickerware manufacturer may include rattan gazebos, peacock chairs, canopied beds, or even a rickshaw.

Rattan can be shaped into chairs, tables, stools, mirror and picture frames, headboards for beds, chests, bookshelves, magazine racks, lampshades, or even a music stand. For a child's room, you can buy an amusing rattan bed with an elephant's head in front, a mattress supported by four giant feet, and a tail trailing behind.

Some wicker furniture is quite inexpensive, while other pieces cost as much as any well-made furniture item with a wooden frame. You can spend anywhere from $15 to $20 for a simple cane chair to as much as $500 for an elaborate sofa.

Another departure from traditional wicker construction is this modern set of living room furniture, lightly styled to set off the plush deep-tufted leather-look cushions. The barrel-shaped coffee table offers strong construction with the same lightness of design.

It you have to furnish a small area, wicker furniture is ideal. Because of its openwork construction, the ensemble looks less massive than ordinary wood or metal furniture. Wicker is easy to care for, and will last indefinitely. Once a year apply a coat of clear lacquer to wicker furniture that you plan to leave outdoors.

Beginning a Comprehensive Discussion of the Subject

In the historical development of window treatments, curtains, curiously enough, made their appearance before window panes. The Egyptians are known to have hung woven mats in front of their windows.

Glass, however, also made a relatively early appearance at windows. Fragments of glass panes fixed in bronze frames have been found in the ruins of Pompeii and in other Roman ruins. Wealthy Romans also used alabaster, translucent marbles, and shell to let light into their dwellings.

Even cursory examination of window design will reveal a building's period and nationality—consider the narrow, pointed windows of medieval castles, the handsome wrought iron screens protecting Spanish windows, the tiny diamond-shaped panes used by early American colonists, the beveled and engraved glass seen in Victorian ornamental windows.

In the seventeenth century, the English adopted an ingenious Dutch design for a sliding sash window, and through the eighteenth century to the present this window has been characteristic of both English and American houses, although casement windows remain popular on the Continent.

During the eighteenth century also, windows got larger, at least in homes of the rich. The Age of Enlightenment evidently craved physical as well as intellectual illumination. In England, sliding sash windows stretched almost from the ceiling to the floor, while in France, architects pierced walls with long rows of graceful doors. Still handmade, glass was comparatively expensive, and only the well-off could afford to replace oiled paper with glass window panes.

With the nineteenth-century development of increasingly mechanized glassmaking, window glass became still cheaper and still more widely available. Victorians replaced multipaned sashes with larger and larger single panes, and in twentieth-century architecture an entire wall of glass is commonplace.

We are indebted to the Victorians also for the invention of the storm window, a demountable extra layer of glass that greatly reduces heat loss in the cooler months.

Window types

Windows can be categorized by the supporting members as double-hung, sliding, casement, hopper, awning, or jalousie. These types can be used in combinations to provide style and/or character, such as french, picture, bay, strip, dormer, glass wall, or clerestory.

■ Double-hung sash window: a window in which two panels slide up and down in vertical grooves, their movements controlled by cords and counterweights concealed in the window jamb. The great advantage of the sliding sash is that the window moves entirely in the plane of the wall, an arrangement that does not expose the open window to breakage.

A popular window type for more than 200 years, the double-hung window is still a stan-

Though the commanding window decoration shown opposite would seem to need no justification, it is in fact an extremely ingenious cover-up for two overlarge windows set too close together. Plywood panels, pierced with Moorish arches, are covered with gold-colored vinyl fabric, and the Hispano-Moresque flavor of the room is carried still further with black braid and ball fringe.

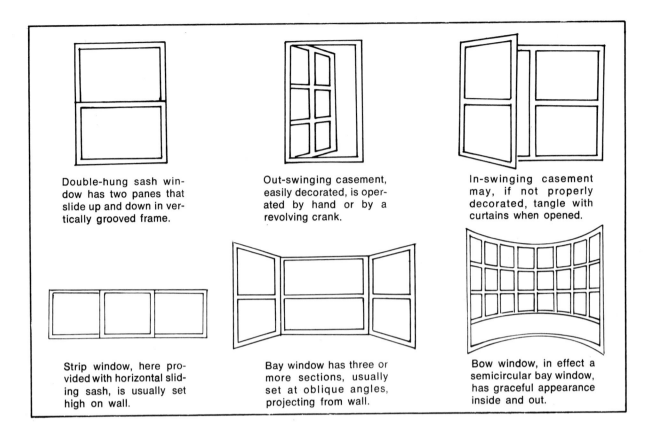

Double-hung sash window has two panes that slide up and down in vertically grooved frame.

Out-swinging casement, easily decorated, is operated by hand or by a revolving crank.

In-swinging casement may, if not properly decorated, tangle with curtains when opened.

Strip window, here provided with horizontal sliding sash, is usually set high on wall.

Bay window has three or more sections, usually set at oblique angles, projecting from wall.

Bow window, in effect a semicircular bay window, has graceful appearance inside and out.

dard article in today's new houses. In some traditional architectural styles of houses, such as the Cape Cod house, double-hung windows usually contain a number of rectangular panes supported by slender wood muntins. These windows are often described by the number of panes in each sash—six-over-four perhaps for a small window or twelve-over-sixteen for a very large one. Today, to simplify washing multipaned windows, manufacturers often equip them with snap-in muntins. These are composed of a wood grid that makes a large pane of glass look like a number of small panes.

Preassembled double-hung windows, comprising frame, cords, and panes all ready to be set into framed openings, are available in assorted sizes and styles and are a generally accepted cost-cutting device in construction.

■ Sliding window: a window with two panes of glass, one or both of which may slide horizontally across the other. Like the double-hung window, it operates within the plane of the wall.

■ Casement window: a hinged window that opens like a door, either in or out, and that operates either by hand or by a crank. Casement windows also have some functional advantages, as when a window opening is too small to accept a double-hung sash. Unlike the double-hung window, only half of which can be opened at any given time, the hinged casement allows the entire area of the window to be opened.

Available with either wood or metal frames, casement windows are also provided with snap-in muntins if you insist on period authenticity. These are rectangular or diamond-shaped.

■ Hopper window: essentially a casement window hinged horizontally. It invariably opens from the top to the inside. In domestic applications, the hopper window is most familiar in basement light wells.

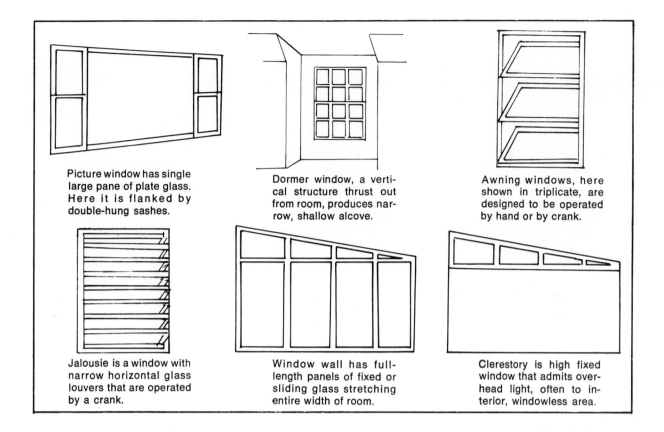

Picture window has single large pane of plate glass. Here it is flanked by double-hung sashes.

Dormer window, a vertical structure thrust out from room, produces narrow, shallow alcove.

Awning windows, here shown in triplicate, are designed to be operated by hand or by crank.

Jalousie is a window with narrow horizontal glass louvers that are operated by a crank.

Window wall has full-length panels of fixed or sliding glass stretching entire width of room.

Clerestory is high fixed window that admits overhead light, often to interior, windowless area.

■ Awning window: similar to the hopper window but opening from the bottom to the outside. Awning windows are often mounted in tiers of three or more panes. A similar window that opens to the inside is commonly called a *projecting* window.

■ Jalousie: constructed of a series of movable glass strips that, operating on the principle of the venetian blind, can be adjusted to admit or exclude air. The jalousie is a very useful device for enclosed porches and winter solaria. The glass is sometimes pebbled or etched to obstruct visual penetration. It is also much used in subtropical sections of the country, where it allows the free circulation of air while blocking out heavy rains.

Special uses of windows

■ French windows: tall double casement windows, opening in the center and extending almost to the floor. To prevent accidental glass breakage, the French window is often protected by a railing—like a small deck—mounted on the outside of the building, and the window must thus open to the inside.

■ Picture window: a large expanse of fixed glass installed to exploit a view. For safety's sake, it is almost always glazed with plate glass. Although some picture windows are provided with muntins, especially in traditional houses, these obviously divide and obscure the picture the window was intended to frame. Most picture windows are therefore constructed of a single large pane.

The picture window enjoyed great vogue in the fifties, and housing developers unfortunately built many picture windows that framed no view at all except the corresponding picture window across the street. These windows present special functional and decorating problems

A sliding glass window-wall, opposite, frames a spectacular view of blooming rhododendrons. This is the sort of outlook that fully warrants an entire wall of glass. The window wall here is treated as an integrated whole, a scallopped and tasseled valance reflecting the edge of the awning outside. The boldly patterned black-and-beige draperies are in keeping with the scale of the room and set off the overall scheme of brilliant primary colors.

In the living room below, tiered windows, framed by softly draped dark green velvet, rise almost to the lofty vaulted ceiling. The top tier, made of random panes of stained glass, filters sunlight into interesting patterns that fall across the living room. The lower tier, the clear panes of its casement windows screened by delicate turned spindles, is provided with roller shades laminated with green velvet, their edge trimmed with green braid.

Semisheer draperies give a boy's bedroom in a city apartment maximum benefit of light. Tailored design, using neat French pleats and straight tiebacks, gets a touch of appropriate decoration from wide black-and-red border trim.

A conventional window is ▶ dramatized with a three-part treatment that includes a fabric-laminated window shade with scalloped Empire hem, framed by vivid green draw curtains on a traverse rod concealed by a black pelmet. White draperies with coordinated black trim hang from wood rings.

that will be discussed and illustrated as special topics throughout this and the next volume.

■ Bay window: a construction with at least three sides that projects from the wall of a house and that has windows on all sides. If the structure is curved, it is often called a *bow* window.

Functionally, the purpose of the bay window is to admit more light than a flush window could do, and it is therefore often seen in city buildings where the size of the exterior wall is limited. Aesthetically, it imparts an appearance of expansive generosity, and it is as attractive in rambling country houses as in the city.

■ Strip window: a long row of rather shallow panes, usually installed at ceiling height. The strip window is a useful device in, say, a front bedroom requiring both light and privacy. The strip window is usually a combination of fixed panes and awning windows. This arrangement is variously known as a ribbon window or a ranch window, the latter often referring to panes set at a conventional height.

■ Dormer window: a vertical window set in a sloping roof and topped by a roof of its own. It may be served by either a double-hung or casement window.

■ Glass wall: an expanse of glass running from floor to ceiling and wall to wall. A hallmark of contemporary architecture, the glass wall combines the functions of wall, window, and door. In most modern installations, the glass is set in fixed and sliding metal frames, but in traditional houses where a glass wall may serve, for example, a backyard terrace, wood frames and hinged doors may be more appropriate.

■ Clerestory: strictly speaking, a window built up above an adjacent roof in order to admit light in a large space. The term is also used in modern building to describe a gable with fixed glazing that serves the same purpose as a strip window.

All glass areas in a house present decorating difficulties of one sort or another. Perhaps the window opens inward, like the hopper window,

and so cannot be operated when curtains are drawn. Perhaps it is awkwardly placed architecturally—like a badly placed bay window. Suggestions for solving these problems will be dealt with later in this article.

Special glazing

To cope with some of the problems presented by the glass wall, glass manufacturers have devised an assortment of special window glasses.

Because sheet glass is a very poor insulator, large areas of glass permit great heat loss. Glass walls should always be double glazed, the two layers of glass sandwiching an insulating layer of air. Double glazing also eliminates moisture condensation that occurs when cold air strikes warm glass. However, you must be careful to install the glass properly. Many manufacturers now offer thermal insulating glass that is sealed on the edges with an air space between two sheets of plate glass. It is available in standard sheet sizes.

Tinted glass, either green or bronze-colored, is often used in modern commercial building to inhibit heat absorption, which places a great burden on air-conditioning equipment. The material is expensive, however, and the color distortion, though slight, makes it generally unappealing in residential building.

Glass used where safety is important is tempered; that is, the molten sheets are subjected to special cooling processes that increase the material's resistance to breakage. For areas particularly threatened by breakage, wire glass—panes in which a layer of wire mesh is embedded—is available. Its appearance is unattractive, however, and its application is generally limited to inconspicuous areas.

A masterly scheme, wholly successful both functionally and aesthetically, treats a row of windows both individually and as an integrated whole. Sheer glass curtains filter daylight for a soft luminescent atmosphere. The exuberant print, needing no further help in making an impression, is draped with simple pleats and tailored tiebacks.

In locations requiring a contradictory combination of visual privacy and adequate light, as next to the front door or in the bathroom, etched or patterned glass can fill both requirements.

Exterior window treatments

A window's reason for being is to furnish a room with light and, secondarily, air. Nothing is perfect, however, and a window will often admit too much light and air, depending upon its orientation and the time of day. In addition, glass, because of its transparency and fragility, offers slight protection against peeping toms and robbers.

To an extent, you can cure these defects on the outside of your house. The devices for exterior light and privacy control are, to be sure, less flexible than those that control illumination from within. They must also be selected with some attention to the house's external appearance—gaily striped canvas awnings, for example, might look completely out of place on the severe form of an avant-garde glass and concrete house

Permanent control of the amount of light, and therefore of heat, striking an area of glass is effected by deep overhangs. This solution must, of course, be provided at the time of construction, but if you are building or remodeling and intend to have large expanses of glass on the west side of the house, an overhang is virtually a must.

Awnings

Awnings offer the same protection as overhangs, and can, besides, be installed above existing windows. Durable, more-or-less-permanent awnings are made of aluminum, or, more durable still, of plastic-coated steel or aluminum. They are available either as fixed installations or in roll-up versions.

These metal awnings do have one flaw. They tend to be rather overwhelming in appearance, and too often are chosen for their utilitarian value only, their aesthetic considerations ignored.

The traditional awning is, of course, the striped or plain canvas awning. To people of a certain age, the appearance of these awnings, as well as the soft filtered light they transmit, has great nostalgic charm.

Although their initial cost is low, canvas awnings do have a great many disadvantages. They are subject to fading by the sun and rotting by the rain. They tear. They must be replaced fairly often. They must be raised and lowered as the sun changes its position, and they must be removed in the fall and rehung in spring.

A medley of white-on-white-on-white, the window treatment is kept suitably simple in a room dominated by flamboyant bedspreads and filigree-patterned wallpaper. Gathered glass curtains, hung at upper and lower sashes, are supplemented by white linen draperies.

In a rather elegant bedroom, formal draperies gathered ▶ on a wood rod are left extralong, allowing a fluid train of green-and-white print to rest on the floor. Tiebacks are knotted high, looping the draperies in a swag effect and allowing the hem to fall in an easy cascade.

Shutters

Although shutters on many modern houses are purely ornamental, they do have a utilitarian purpose, especially in areas of the country where the sunshine is bright. Plain paneled shutters offer only an either/or method of light control: either they admit all light when open or exclude all light when shut. Louvered shutters, however, allow you to adjust the light level with some precision. Adjustable louvers, on the other hand, are rather more difficult to clean and paint than are plain shutters.

For a more detailed discussion, see the article *Shutters,* Vol. 15, p. 2858.

Grilles

To ensure privacy at the front of the house or at a window uncomfortably close to a neighboring house, you can fill the window frame with a fixed lattice or pierced screen. Trellised panels and filligreed plywood in a variety of patterns are usually available at good-sized lumberyards.

The patterned openings of screens must be small if they are to provide much privacy, particularly at night; and this will necessitate the sacrifice of some natural light. These screens also must be carefully chosen to suit the design of your house.

The fixed iron grille is an accepted device for protecting windows at sidewalk level in town houses. Their installation is expensive, but, since the grilles are embedded directly in the face of the building, they are invincible to all but the most determined assault. Despite their seeming delicacy, iron grilles also provide psychological security.

Iron grilles, when well designed, also have an ornamental function, most especially in the case

A row of crisply tailored draperies emphasizes the strict rhythm of a wall of tall single-paned casement windows. The box-pleated draperies, made of white linen, are hung from a black wood rod by fabric loops cut and sewn at the exact width and spacing of the pleats. The tiebacks are fastened precisely at the level of the window sills.

of Spanish-style houses. Carved wood grilles, although admittedly offering minimal protection, are frequently used as decorative exterior window treatments in Spanish architecture.

Although one can hardly think of them as "grilles," well-placed trees and shrubs make very effective screens for windows. Planted where their shade falls across the window, they provide all the protection from the direct rays of the sun provided by structural sunshades. The massing of their foliage and their pleasant dappled shadows, in addition, soften the lines of the house and enhance its texture.

Interior window treatments

The primary reasons for hanging any material in front of a window are functional—to control light, to provide insulation, and to ensure privacy.

Light control may simply require that sunlight be limited in the early morning or late afternoon so that the level of illumination is comfortable for the room's occupants, or to prevent fading of carpets and upholstery fabrics. In the bedroom, you may want to exclude morning light entirely.

Before window glass became a commonly available building material, fabric hangings served as screens to keep the cold winter winds outside. Now they are often used to keep the expensively heated or cooled air inside.

Considerable heat loss does occur at windows, either through leakage around the sashes or through the glass itself. Good weatherstripping will prevent leakage, while double glazing serves as insulation. Nonetheless, curtains and shutters still offer a useful second line of de-

This bay window becomes a private nook in the evening when the blinds are drawn. The tightly gathered white draperies (actually king-size bed sheets) are tied at sofa level to reveal tall triangles of emphatically striped shades.

fense, besides eliminating the irritating thermal eddies that are inevitable around windows.

Ordinarily you will not need protection from prying eyes in the daytime unless the window is located right at the sidewalk where passing strangers might have a fairly good view into the house. At night, however, when it is brighter inside than out, you can make privacy certain by drawing thick draperies or by closing venetian blinds.

A bare glass window at night, in any case, presents the appearance, from inside, of a blank, black hole that must be covered in some way. More importantly, perhaps, these nighttime screens provide psychological assurance. Most people harbor lingering fears of what might be "out there" in the dark, so that even urbanites living on the twentieth floor of an apartment building will often draw the curtains after dark.

Decorative aspects

Even if draperies had no functional justification, it is likely, given the human taste for embellishment, that most people would ornament their windows. For one thing, the strict rectangular lines of the window frame seem to call for a

◄ The prettiest, cheeriest, and most suitable curtains for the kitchen are also the simplest and the easiest to make. The casing and small heading require only straight machine stitching—even the hems, if you are not finicky about a fine finish, can be machine-sewn. The kitchen curtains shown here, as well as the perky ruffled valance topping them, were made with a permanent-press fabric.

An extra length of upholstery fabric was laminated to the living room blinds shown here for a coordinated deco-rating scheme. The scheme is also enhanced by the un-usual quartet of tiebacks mounted on wood medallions.

In a citified kitchen that is anything but quaint, the window over the sink is hung with black velveteen curtains trimmed with thick red cotton cording. The window shade, no less sophisticated, is red-and-white-striped; its pull, a black curtain rod, is supported by matching loops.

Cheerful coin-dotted cotton curtains border a harmonizing window shade, and the entire composition is capped by a coordinated valance. The scalloped lower edges of both shade and valance are made of the curtain material; overlapping scallops are decorated with individual coin cutouts.

Woolen hangings, draped in the Victorian manner, frame a playful drawing of a bird in a gilded cage. The elaborate heading flanks a graceful swag with symmetrical jabots. These are trimmed, as is the shaped edge of the shade with typically Victorian tasseled fringe.

softening effect. The heavy pediments and fine carving that framed windows in the seventeenth and eighteenth centuries supplied this need and were, furthermore, handsome enough to stand on their own. The simple window frames of today, however, offer no such visual splendor and fairly invite enrichment.

For another thing, bright light naturally attracts the eye, and the window therefore seems an ideal place to make a decorating statement. Light itself—trickling through gauzy fabric, washing the ranked tops of open louvers, silhouetting the outlines of a striking pattern— gives lasting enjoyment to the eye.

Window decoration, whether curtains, blinds, or shutters, is often the first thing a visitor notices as he enters a room. Nevertheless, windows are, as a rule, a secondary decorating area, following the lead of furniture and walls in style and color.

With curtains you can establish a totally integrated decorating scheme, as when draperies, wall coverings, and upholstery are all of the same fabric. Or you might pick up a subordinate color from a rich print—pink, say—and use it as a subtle counterpoint to the main theme, perhaps hanging deep rose draperies over pale pink shades. Or you can create a particular mood, as diaphanous white curtains in a dressing room would convey a feeling of delicate femininity, or sober monk's-cloth draperies in a gentleman's study would establish an ambience of sober masculinity.

In a large, formal, and expensively furnished room, you might cover the window with successive layers of glass curtains and velvet overdraperies. More elaborately still, you might frame this composition with draped velvet swags at the cornice and cascading falls of velvet down the sides. (It is just conceivable that an interior decorator with flair and monumental self-assurance would successfully combine all these elements.)

At the other extreme, in an avant-garde modern setting, you might dispense with window decoration altogether. If the house has been

In an unexpected application, ball fringes become soft bead hangings in this girl's bedroom. The material, available ready-made, is prestrung on fiber-glass cord. Strings of fringe, in a pleasing combination of red, pink, and orange, are suspended above window and bed.

Outlined with a blue-black frame, this window has been given a beautifully simple treatment: a cascade of sheer white curtains that falls in classic folds, accented at the top by an elegantly draped swag of dark purple velvet.

properly designed and oriented, additional light and privacy control should be unnecessary. The softening effect of gathered fabric may, further, strike a discordant note in an interior designed around strict geometrical forms and hard shiny surfaces. The big glass areas so characteristic of modern architecture are often unadorned so as not to interfere with the clean lines of the structure or with the view.

To replace the bleakness of dark glass at night, well-designed lighting of trees and plantings can transform a black mirror into a lovely mural. (See *Outdoor Lighting,* Vol. 13, p. 2324.)

In between these extremes, there is an enormous number of possible window decorations: pretty ruffled curtains for a nursery, bright un-pretentious café curtains in a kitchen, dark-stained shutters in a semiformal living room.

Window treatments can also serve what might be called functional decoration by visually correcting badly proportioned or awkwardly spaced windows. The solution might be as straightforward as simply concealing all the windows behind long pinch-pleated draperies, or as sophisticated as constructing fabric-covered framing panels that create an illusion of uniformity and regularity. Typical problem windows will be taken up later in this article.

The discussion of windows, dealing more specifically with particular decorative treatments such as curtains, shades, and shutters, will be resumed in the succeeding volume.

Master/Guide

Tempera

Colors produced by mixing powders and egg yolks. The resulting paste is thinned with water. Traditionally, tempera painting was done on a plaster (gesso) surface. Although the effect resembles oil painting, the tempera color is capable of a more brilliant surface. The technique of tempera painting has been popular since the Middle Ages and it is similar to the modern technique of *gouache* painting.

Tenon

In woodworking, the projecting portion of a mortise and tenon joint. To form this joint, a ledge (tenon) at the end of one board is fitted into a channel (mortise) formed at the end of another board. For more information on woodworking joints, see *Woods,* Vol. 18.

Tent (or Field) Bed

A lightly scaled eighteenth-century bed surmounted by a graceful canopy (tester) fixed to the bed's four posts and in form suggesting a tent. The design was developed from the earlier field (or campaign) bed intended as a portable piece of military equipment. Campaign furniture has recently been revived. For examples, see *Campaign Furniture,* Vol. 4, p. 689.

Term (or Terminal Figure)

A furniture support, often in the form of a figure modeled in somewhat grotesque style, popular during the Renaissance and later Empire periods. The name is sometimes applied more precisely to a pedestal in the form of a bust that tapers to a wide base or splayed feet.

Tern Foot

An eighteenth-century French scrolled foot often placed on a cabriole leg. The tern foot, formed of three scrolls, sometimes resting on a small protective pad, was a more ornate version of the scroll, or French whorl, foot.

Terrace

A term broadly applied to an outdoor area adjoining a house or apartment. The terrace area is frequently defined by a low fence or wall. For a discussion of the decorative treatments of terraces, see *Outdoor Living,* Vol. 13, p. 2332; and *Patios,* Vol. 14, p. 2546.

Terra-Cotta

A coarse and porous baked clay varying in color from red to dull tan. Terra-cotta (fired with or without a glaze) has been commonly used since ancient times for making artistic as well as utilitarian objects.

A Cretan terra-cotta piece modeled as a double vessel in the shape of an animal. Body of piece is unglazed.

Terrazzo

A surfacing material composed of crushed marble blended into cement, then polished. Due to the coloring of the marble, terrazzo forms a highly decorative surface suitable for walls, floors, and other walkways.

Terry Clock

A variety of inexpensive wooden mantel clock named after its American designer, Eli Terry (1772-1852). Similar to the pillar-and-scroll clock, the Terry clock featured a scrolled and broken pediment, columns on either side of the glass-closed face, small bracket feet descending from a curved apron, and wooden (instead of metal) clockworks.

Tertiary Color

A color produced by mixing a primary color with a neighboring secondary color on the color wheel. For more information about color and the proper use of the color wheel, see *Color,* Vol. 5, p. 842.

Tessellated (and Tesserae)

The term used to describe a surface covered with a mosaic. The mosaic (or tessellated) surface is composed of small bits of material (such as glass, stone, metal) known as *tesserae.* This

A mosaic portrait of Saint Augustine—a detail of the Palatine Chapel dome in Palermo, Sicily.

form of wall and floor treatment is very ancient, and unusually beautiful examples of portraits and patterns survive from both ancient and more modern times. For a discussion of mosaics, see *Crafts,* Vol. 6, p. 998.

Tester

The canopy suspended over a four-poster bed. One of the original purposes of the tester was to hold up the fabrics dropped to prevent drafts when the bed was in use. However, this functional purpose soon was subordinated and the tester became the subject of lavish decorative treatments. The style of the tester varied greatly, usually conforming to the tastes of the period.

Tete D'Ange

A sculptured representation of an angel, usually in the form of a bust with stylized spreading wings. It was often used as a decorative support in the manner of a console.

Texture

In decorating, the term for the tactile and visual qualities of a surface; for example, satin has a smooth texture and concrete has a rough one. For a discussion of the decorative values of different textures, see *Textures,* p. 3075.

Theorem Painting

A painting rendered on velvet or a similar material by means of a stencil. Theorem paintings were a popular art form during the early decades of the nineteenth century.

Thomas, Seth (1785-1859)

American clock designer associated with the renowned clockmaker Eli Terry. Thomas worked chiefly in Connecticut, a center of clock manufacturing during the nineteenth century.

Thomire, Pierre Phillipe (1751-1843)

French metalworker (*ciseleur*) and engraver noted for his delicate bronze furniture mounts in the Louis XVI and French Empire styles.

Thonet, Michael (1796-1871)

Austrian furniture designer and manufacturer responsible for the mass production and consequent vast distribution of bentwood furniture during the middle of the nineteenth century. By means of steam and pressure, Thonet bent round strips of wood into simple but elegant curved forms. This technique has had a permanent influence upon modern furniture styles, particularly in the design of chairs. Among the best-known examples of Thonet's work are the bentwood rocker and Vienna café chair. For information and illustrations, see *Modern Furniture,* Vol. 12, p. 2208.

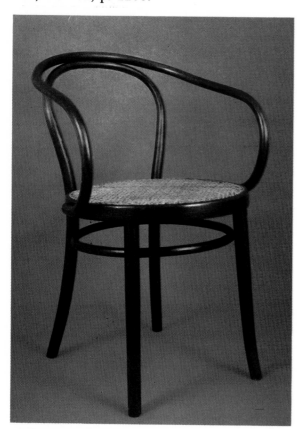

The curving lines and simple airy designs of Michael Thonet's furniture have made it perennially popular.

Threaded Glass

A sixteenth-century form of Venetian glass characterized by threads (or canes) of glass manipulated into lacelike patterns and enclosed in clear glass. The technique, known in ancient times, reached its highest development among the Renaissance Venetian artisans. Threaded glass is also known as *lace glass.*

Three-Back Windsor Chair

A style of Windsor chair back with a crest formed by another, miniature, back. The crest functioned as a headrest. This type of Windsor chair is also known as a *comb back.* American and English Windsor chairs share the same features: spindles closing back and arms, splayed legs, and scooped seats.

Thumb Glass

A large goblet that has indentations arranged around the base of the bowl in order to help the drinker hold the glass with a steady hand.

Thumbpiece (or Purchase)

A knob, variously fashioned, set near the hinge on the lid of a handled mug or tankard. When holding the tankard by the handle, the drinker's thumb was free to raise or lower the lid by means of this knob.

Thuya

A hard reddish wood found in Africa. During the eighteenth century, particularly in England, thuya was favored as a veneer.

Ticking

A strong, heavy cotton fabric usually woven into colored stripes. Ticking is used for upholstery, wall coverings, and mattress covers.

Tieback

A decorative device, such as a cord or hook, used near the middle of a window drapery to hold back the fabric. See *Windows and Window Treatments,* p. 3152; and Vol. 18.

Tiffany, Louis Comfort (1848-1933)

Innovative and influential American glass designer, director of the famous Tiffany Glass and

In addition to his stained-glass works, Tiffany also created articles of favrile glass.

Decorating Company. Foremost American practitioner of the Art Nouveau style, Tiffany (among other accomplishments) introduced favrile glass, an iridescent colored glass with gracefully flowing patterns. Also interested in mosaic techniques, Tiffany produced lamps, today immensely popular and somewhat scarce, composed of patterns and motifs arranged from small colored glass pieces held together by lead strips in the manner of stained glass.

Tigerwood
A hard brown native African wood, similar to walnut. Tigerwood is marked with black streaks, a characteristic from which it derives its name. It is favored for paneling and veneers.

Tile
A thin plate of varied size, shape, and material used as the basic unit in covering surfaces such as floors, walls, and roofs.

Tiling
A surface covering of tiles, generally used on floors and walls. For a discussion of tiling materials and installations, see *Tiling*, p. 3082.

Tint
The term used to refer to a paler color produced by adding white to a brighter hue. The term is used in contrast to "shade," which refers to a color darkened by the addition of black. For more information, see *Color*, Vol. 5, p. 842.

Tintype (or Ferrotype)
A photograph produced on a lacquered iron plate. The technique, now obsolete, was popular during the late nineteenth century for the taking of souvenir snapshots.

Tobacco Box
A small elegant lidded silver container, fashionable during the eighteenth century for holding tobacco. Although similar to the snuffbox, the tobacco box was larger, deeper, and less ornate.

Toby Jug
An eighteenth-century Staffordshire ceramic mug or pitcher in the form of a seated man who is either drinking or holding a pipe. The figure wears a hat, the top of which provides the opening of the pitcher.

Toile (and Toile de Jouy)
A French term broadly used to refer to the pattern appearing on printed fabrics. (The word "toile" actually means "cloth".) Toile de Jouy translates as cloth of Jouy (a French town near Versailles) and originally described a distinctive eighteenth-century pictorial fabric design printed in muted tones devised by the celebrated cloth printer and dyer Philip Oberkampf.

Tole
Objects, such as lampshades, vases, boxes, and trays, made from painted tin. Painted tinware was popular during the nineteenth century.

Tongue and Groove
An ancient device for joining two pieces of wood by inserting a tongue (a projecting ledge) of

one piece into a groove (a fitted cavity) of the other piece. This joint, somewhat similar to the *mortise and tenon,* may be reinforced by glue or by a pin inserted so as to pass through both pieces of wood. The joint was often used in the construction of chairs, tables, and cabinets. For more information on woodworking joints, see *Woods,* Vol. 18.

Torchere (or Gueridon)
A tall slender stand used to hold a large candle or candelabrum. French baroque examples were very ornately carved and gilded.

A lavishly ornamented torchère from a sixteenth-century cathedral in Venice. The materials are bronze and marble.

Torsade
A semicircular molding with a twisted appearance suggesting a rope. The torsade is also known as a cable molding.

Tortoiseshell
The outer shell of the tortoise, particularly the hawksbill turtle. During the eighteenth century, tortoiseshell was often used in marquetry work, especially in France. The shell, when not dyed, is semitransparent, darkly mottled, and capable of a brilliant finish. The term is also used to refer to an amber-colored art glass manufactured in America during the nineteenth century.

Tournay (or Tournai) Porcelain
Soft-paste porcelain produced at Tournay, Belgium, during the eighteenth and nineteenth centuries. The best examples were in the rococo style popularized by Meissen.

Townsend, Job (1699-1765)
Foremost member of a renowned family of cabinetmakers who worked in Newport, R.I., during the eighteenth and early nineteenth centuries. Furniture designed in Newport achieved such a distinctive excellence that it is considered, along with the products of the Philadelphia school, to be among the finest furniture manufactured in America.

Tracery
The decorative and symmetrical subdivision of windows, particularly the stained-glass windows of medieval Gothic architecture. The tracery patterns of these windows were complex and of the highest form of artistry. Among the best

known of the patterns was the clover shape composed of a varied number of lobes (or petals). This shape appeared in trefoils (three lobes), quatrefoils (four lobes), and cinquefoils (five lobes). The trefoil and quatrefoil motifs were also used as carved forms on medieval furniture.

Trailed Circuit

A chain motif applied to glassware, particularly in England. The motif was usually composed of two strips of glass meeting at regular intervals and trailed around the glass, thus suggesting a chain applied in a circuit.

Transfer Printing

A simple and inexpensive technique used to decorate pottery, especially in eighteenth- and nineteenth-century England and America. The image to be transferred was impressed on paper from an engraved metal plate that had been coated with suitable colors; it was then transferred from the paper to the ceramic surface. In some cases, the image was also hand painted.

Transom

A term broadly used to refer to a hinged section, generally of glass panels, placed above a door in order to permit circulation of air when the door is closed.

Trauschein

The German word for a marriage certificate. Documents of this type, as well as others, were often artfully embellished by the Pennsylvania Dutch in a decorative calligraphy called *fractur schrift*. The *fractur* art took in both writing (derived from medieval Gothic script) and stylized pictorial patterns, often of unusual artistry. Bold colors and strong designs such as hearts, birds, tulips, and trees illustrated these documents.

Travertine

A light-colored marble, as well as other stone of similar mineral content, with a rough texture created by its pockmarked surface. The term is also used to describe a vinyl tile manufactured to resemble the stone.

Trayle

A continuous motif composed of vines, leaves, and grapes. The carved motifs were often used on Elizabethan and Jacobean furniture and paneling.

Tree of Life

A decorative motif inherited from ancient times and common in Near Eastern as well as European art. Although it varies in form, degree of stylization, and complexity of design, the general features are constant; they present a tree with leaves and flowers interspersed with docile animals. In American art the tree-of-life motif often appears in the *fractur* art of the Pennsylvania Dutch.

Trenail

A wooden nail (or *tree nail*). Trenails were made from hard woods, sharpened to a point, and dried and compressed. Once in place, when moistened, they swelled to fit tightly.

Trencher (and Trencher Salt)

The English term for an early form of dinner plate. The original trenchers were slabs of bread upon which meat was served at table. In the sixteenth century, the trencher developed from a square piece of flat wood to a round wood or metal plate. The trencher salt was any bowl, dish, or other container for salt that accompanied each trencher when dining.

Trestle Table

A large rectangular dining table supported on a trestle framework composed of two upright standards joined by a single stretcher bar. During the Middle Ages, the trestle table was constructed so that the top could be removed and the standards folded against the stretcher. Tables of similar construction but more ornate decoration were also common during the Renaissance; an American version, known as the *sawbuck table*, was frequently found in colonial homes.

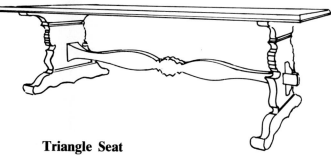

Triangle Seat

A small chair (of Scandinavian origin) with triangular seat and a simple back; the apex of the triangle was intended to fit into a corner. During the eighteenth century, the design was refined and the chair acquired curved arms and a more elaborately formed back.

Tricoteuse

An eighteenth- and nineteenth-century French worktable similar to contemporary English and American sewing tables. Although the general outline varied, the tricoteuse was lightly scaled and equipped with small drawers or convenient recesses for storing materials.

Trictrac (or Backgammon) Table

A popular eighteenth-century gaming table first introduced in France. The typical trictrac table was rectangular with a removable top surface often covered in leather or baize. When removed, the top exposed a sunken trictrac board (similar to a checkerboard) and other accouterments required for playing. The trictrac table was a forerunner of the modern card table.

Tridarn (or Welsh) Cupboard

A large wooden cupboard that originated in Wales during the seventeenth century. The tridarn cupboard was composed of three parts: a large lower unit with two doors, a recessed middle unit with three doors, and an open shelf above for the display of plate. The cupboard was decorated with simple carving and paneling on the sides and doors. Variations of the design can be found among the Pennsylvania Welsh settlers.

Trim

A term broadly used to refer to decorative aspects of interior construction, such as moldings, or of exterior construction, such as shutters.

Trimming

An accessory of a decorative nature that is not strictly necessary but whose addition provides a fillip to another item. For a discussion of the use of trimmings in decoration of the home, see *Trimmings,* p. 3090.

Tripod Table

A small side table of varied form popular during the eighteenth century. The tripod table usually had a round or polygonal top resting on a pedestal supported by three splayed legs. Among the best-known examples of this design are the piecrust and tilt-top tables. The piecrust table (also often constructed with a tilt top) was supported by a central carved pedestal rising from three cabriole legs. The table received its name from the scalloped gallery (similar to the pinched edges of pies) around the tabletop.

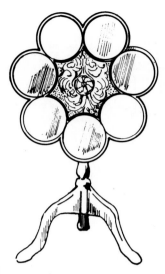

Triptych

Originally, a medieval religious painting rendered on three hinged panels. The term is also applied to a mirror or screen in the same form.

Trivet

A small platform of varied design and material, slightly raised by tiny legs and intended to support hot pans, serving dishes, a pressing iron, etc., above a table or similar surface. Trivets, usually with a handle, were introduced during the eighteenth century; they were often made of openwork cast iron or of ceramic tiles embedded in a wooden frame.

Trompe l'Oeil

In painting, the art of representing objects with such accurate and ingenious perspective and foreshortening as to convince the eye of the observer to accept depth of space on a flat surface. The term *trompe l'oeil* actually means in French "fool the eye." Known since ancient times, this style of painting has been used on murals and ceramics as well as canvas, and its popularity in European art is thought to have originated with the Italian Renaissance painters, particularly the della Robbia school. In modern interior design, trompe l'oeil effects are used to expand inner space by suggesting depth. For a discussion, see *Trompe l'Oeil,* p. 3100; and *Walls and Wall Coverings,* p. 3152.

An eighteenth-century trompe l'oeil group by C.W. Peale. The painting is said to have deceived George Washington, who nodded absentmindedly to the "boys" as he passed.

Trophy

An ornamental motif composed of armorial elements, weapons, leaves, flowers, musical instruments, or similar objects arranged with festooned fabrics in a balanced manner against a wall. The term is also applied to such a motif when used in paintings or tapestries.

Trumpet Leg

A turned leg, popular during the William and Mary period in English furniture, that has an outline suggestive of a turned-up trumpet. This elaborate leg is often found on highboys and tables as well as chairs and settees.

Trundle (or Truckle) Bed

A small, low bed, originally of medieval design, that could be rolled about on wheels. The trundle bed, considered a child's bed in later periods, was usually stored beneath a larger, higher bed. A common household piece during the American colonial period, this bed is the forerunner of the modern hideaway bed.

Tub Chair (and Tub Sofa)

An eighteenth-century and early-nineteenth-century English chair with a rounded back (like one end of a tub) and prominent arms. The design is similar to the spoon-back chair of the same period. Associated with French design, the tub sofa was a large upholstered settee with a bean shape that thus allowed the sitters to turn comfortably towards each other during conversation. This sofa usually had arms provided with small upholstered pads.

Tucker Porcelain

American hard-bone porcelain manufactured in Philadelphia by William Ellis Tucker during the early part of the nineteenth century. The wares, apart from patriotic decorative motifs and portraits, resembled those of the renowned French Sèvres products. Customary decorations included floral patterns and gilt trim.

Tudor Furniture Style

English furniture styles associated with the reigns of the Tudor monarchs (1485-1558) until the time of Elizabeth I (1558-1603). A period of transition, Tudor styles reveal a mixed Gothic and Renaissance sensibility: a preference for carved wood but restrained decorative details; Gothic architectural forms, but classical decorative motifs. During the reign of Elizabeth, Italian Renaissance styles strongly imposed their influence upon English design and the term English Renaissance properly dates from this period.

Tudor Rose

A carved rose motif associated with the English Tudor dynasty (1485-1558). The motif featured five opened petals surrounding a smaller rose and originally symbolized the reconciliation of the houses of York and Lancaster that brought an end to the Wars of the Roses.

Tulip Motif

A stylized tulip of varied form popular in European and American arts since the introduction of this Oriental flower during the sixteenth century. In America, the tulip was a favorite decoration on the furniture and pottery of the Pennsylvania Dutch and, as a consequence, Pennsylvania Dutch pottery was known as tulipware.

Tulipwood

The white soft wood of the American tulip tree. Often used in American woodworking, this wood fades with age to a yellow shade. The name tulipwood is also applied to a reddish wood found in Brazil, often favored as a veneer.

Tulle

Originally a simple, but extremely fine, form of lace having a light, dense, unadorned mesh. It is thought to have been first made in the French town of Tulle. By extension, tulle today is a sheer net, frequently sized to stiffen it, used for veils, tutus, etc.

Tunbridge Veneer

A patterned veneer produced at Tunbridge Wells, England, during the nineteenth century. The technique involved in the construction of the veneer was similar to that employed by Venetian artisans in the production of millefiori glass: thin strips of differently colored woods in a natural state were glued together vertically, thus forming a block with a top surface showing the intended pattern. Then the block was cut horizontally, producing a series of veneers with the same pattern. The veneer, after it was applied to the furniture surface, was brought to a high finish. Also known as "English mosaics," Tunbridge veneers required unusually fine craftsmanship. For more information about furniture veneers, see *Veneering,* p. 3142.

Tureen

A large covered bowl originally intended for serving soup. During the seventeenth and eighteenth centuries, the soup tureen was made of silver or porcelain and was often shaped with great artistry. The tureen usually had four stubby legs, a handle on either side, and a decorative knob on the cover.

A Strasbourg ceramic tureen in the shape of a turkey. The piece dates from the eighteenth century.

Turkish (or Cozy) Corner

An alcove or room area furnished and decorated in a manner that suggested the styles of the Near East, especially Turkey. A whimsical predilection of the Victorian period, the Turkish corner was often appointed with an overstuffed daybed, a Turkish rug, bright cushions, small tables carved in an Eastern manner, and other furnishings that might evoke the exotic atmosphere of the Levant.

Turkish Rug

The common name for all handwoven rugs from the Near East (or Asia Minor). The rugs are made from a variety of materials and in a variety of designs and colors. Oriental rugs are divided into six major categories: Turkoman, Caucasian, Turkish, Persian, Chinese, and Indian. For a discussion and further illustrations, see *Oriental Rugs,* Vol. 12, p. 2282.

Bergama Turkish rug. Often called a Holbein rug, this type of carpet features a design of octagons within squares.

Turning

A process of shaping strips of solid wood into continuous unbroken ornamental designs by cutting the wood with various tools while it turns on a lathe. Turned wood is traditionally used (according to prevailing styles) for chair and table legs, stretcher bars, chair-back spindles, and similar furniture parts. The style of turning is usually referred to by the name of the object that the shape resembles: for example, in English furniture the balloon common on Elizabethan table legs is known as a "melon bulb" turning, and the flaring common on William and Mary legs is known as a "trumpet" turning.

Turnip Dome (and Foot)

A pointed dome usually found on a slender tower and characteristic of the traditional religious architecture of Russia and the Near East. The turnip foot has a ball at its base, rising in a slender curved neck. The general shape is like that of a bottle or tenpin.

Turquoise

An eighteen-century French sofa designed in imitation of the Turkish divan. The turquoise had no back but was formed with two high, broadly scrolled end arms of equal height. Tubular bolsters were nested against the arms, and pillows were placed against the wall against which the turquoise was usually set. The sofa's name goes back to the French word for Turkish.

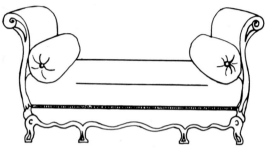

Tweed

A woolen fabric, rough and generally unfinished, woven either in patterned or plain weaves. Tweeds are used for clothing, frequently for outerwear because of their weight.

Twill

A fabric woven in a twill weave. Also the weave itself, where the filling threads cross over one warp thread and under the next two or more threads, to produce the effect of fine diagonal stripes. The twill weave is often used for tweeds.

Two-Chair-Back Settee

A seventeenth- and eighteenth-century wooden settee styled to appear as two armchairs joined into a single unit. The settee thus had five legs (three in front and two in back), and two arms (one on either end), and two splats (one on each back). The two-chair-back settee was also known as a courting chair.

Unicorn

A legendary beast resembling a white horse with a single horn projecting from its forehead. During the Middle Ages, the unicorn was accepted as symbol of Christ and, as a motif, the animal often appears in medieval religious art. In this aspect, the best-known examples are the Unicorn Tapestries now hanging in the Cloisters in New York City.

Last panel of Unicorn Tapestry cycle, depicting the unicorn in captivity. Floral design is called *millefleurs*.

Upholstery

The methods (and the materials) used in stuffing an article of furniture and covering it with a suitable material. Upholstered furniture was rare during the Middle Ages and early Renaissance and included only such small articles as stool and chair seats. However, during the eighteenth century, particularly in France and England, the art of upholstering was greatly refined and skillfully upholstered furniture covered with needlework fabrics became more common. For more information, see *Upholstering,* p. 3104.

Urbino

During the sixteenth and seventeenth centuries, a major center in the production of Italian majolica wares, pottery brilliantly colored by means of tin glazes. During the Renaissance, majolica tablewares, chiefly used as decorative accessories, were adorned with pictorial scenes and intricate arabesques. The colors employed were usually limited to blue, orange, purple, green, and black. The pottery receives its name from the island of Majorca, a port of call for ships from the Mediterranean area.

Urn (and Urn-Splat)

A large vase usually of pottery or metal. Although covered urns were designed as knife holders during the eighteenth century, the urn was traditionally a decorative article, often set upon a stand intended for its display. Common during the eighteenth century in Queen Anne and Chippendale styles, the urn splat was a central urn-shaped chair back usually set in a curved frame.

Vacation Home

That home away from home that so many people long to own. For a thorough discussion of how to go about acquiring, furnishing, and decorating one, see *Vacation Homes,* p. 3118.

Vaisselier-Buffet (and -Horloge)

A French Provincial cabinet constructed in two units: a lower chest closed by two paneled doors, and an upper series of shelves set back from the chest. The shelves were each fronted by a small spindle-formed gallery that functioned to secure leaning plates displayed on the shelves. The general design was derived from the rococo style of Louis XV. The vasselier-horloge differed from the vaisselier-buffet in that it featured a narrow vertical clock set in the central facade of the upper shelves. Both of these pieces, found throughout France (sometimes with different names), are considered unusually fine examples of French Provincial furniture.

Valance

The fabric used like a cornice to hide the tops of draperies. For a discussion, see *Draperies,* Vol. 7, p. 1224; and *Windows and Window Treatments,* p. 3228 and Vol. 18. Another common type of valance is the decorative border of fabric around a bed from mattress to floor that hides the space below.

Van De Velde, Henry (1863-1957)

Belgian architect, furniture designer, and artist influential in the development of modern furniture styles as later exemplified in the work of the German Bauhaus group. For a discussion, see *Modern Furniture,* Vol. 12, p. 2208.

Vargueno

A Spanish Renaissance portable drop-front desk in the shape of a large rectangle supported on a table (known as a *puente* stand). The interior was composed of many small drawers placed around a central cabinet, all intended to hold documents or writing materials. In characteristic Spanish style, the inner facades were richly and boldly carved in geometric motifs, and the *puente* stand was often elaborate and deeply carved and turned or embellished with wrought-iron underbracing.

Varnish

A liquid applied to wood surfaces to produce a glossy transparent finish. Varnish is composed of oils containing dissolved gums or resins. For more information, see *Finishes and Refinishing,* Vol. 8, p. 1366.

Vellum

Originally the inner skin of a calf, lamb, or kid cleaned and treated so as to make it a suitable surface for writing. In contemporary usage, the term vellum is applied to a somewhat brittle semitransparent paper. Vellum was also known as parchment.

Velvet (and Velveteen)

A fabric having a soft heavy short pile, used both for clothing and upholstery. Woven in plain or patterned forms, velvet is made of filaments of silk, nylon, cotton, or rayon, etc. The pile in velvet is composed of warp threads. Velveteen, made of cotton as an imitation velvet, is used for clothing and its pile is derived from weft or filling threads.

Veneering

The art of covering furniture surfaces with thin sheets of wood, usually selected for their more decorative appearance. Introduced from France and Holland, veneers became common on English furniture during the early part of the eighteenth century, particularly in the William and Mary period. Forming patterns with veneers became a special talent of the Georgian period. During the Victorian period, machine-made veneers were used to cover poor wood and consequently veneered furniture came to be considered poor furniture, which had not been the case in the past. Contemporary wood furniture

An elaborately inlaid detail of a chest, the marquetry work of the master Giuseppe Magglioni (1738-1814).

is almost entirely veneered, and the term in no way connotes inferior quality currently. For further information, see *English Styles,* Vol. 7, p. 1266; and *Veneers,* p. 3142.

Venetian Blind (and Jalousie)

A panel or window hanging made of slats of wood or metal that as a unit rotate outward or inward in order to control visibility and air circulation. The forerunner of the venetian blind was the jalousie, a fixed vertical blind or shutter made of a series of slats sloping outward to prevent the entrance of rain or wind and yet permit light. In the nineteenth century, craftsmen perfected the jalousie so that the slats, by means of cords and tape, turned both inward and outward and could be raised and lowered.

Venetian Glass

Remarkably decorative and delicate glass produced in Venice and the adjoining island of Murano, especially since the early Renaissance. Venetian glass, such as millefiori, latticinio, fondi d'oro, and aventurine, was the finest decorative glass in Europe until the introduction of crystal in England during the eighteenth century.

This eighteenth-century Venetian glass tumbler is adorned with an enameled figure of Rebecca at the well.

Venetian Painted Furniture

Rococo furniture made by Venetian craftsmen primarily during the middle of the eighteenth century. Although the style derives from France, the Venetian designs were uniquely delicate and the furniture was painted with an artistry without parallel in Europe. Often, the furniture was first covered with a coating of gesso (plaster) and then decorated with pictures and motifs.

Ventilation

The provision of clean and healthful air within the home and the means whereby it is provided. For a discussion, see *Ventilation,* p. 3148.

Verdigris

The greenish discoloration that sometimes appears on copper, brass, bronze, or other alloys of copper.

Vergeboard (or Bargeboard)

In domestic architecture, the decorative valance-like board running along the edge of a pitched roof, especially over a gable. During the nineteenth century, this board was often cut into continuous lacelike patterns.

Vernis Martin

An unusually fine lacquer perfected in France during the eighteenth century by the Martins, a family of distinguished artists and furniture decorators. Vernis (French: varnish) Martin was greenish in color.

Victorian Furniture Styles

The furniture styles of nineteenth-century England, prevailing from roughly 1837-1901 (the duration of the reign of Queen Victoria). Victorian furniture tended to be of disparate styles, modeling itself upon different strains from the past: rococo, Gothic, and early Renaissance. However, Victorian furniture typically tended to be overdecorated and, when upholstered, overstuffed. See *English Styles,* Vol. 7, p. 1266; and *Furniture Styles,* Vol. 9, p. 1626.

Vile, William (died 1767)

One of the finest furniture designers and cabinetmakers in English history. Cabinetmaker to King George III, Vile produced elegantly proportioned and vigorously carved furniture in a rococo style.

Vinaigrette

A tiny lidded silver or gold container of varied form. The vinaigrette held, behind a pierced-work fitting, a sponge saturated with aromatic vinegar or salts, which liquid was to drive away any tendency to faintness. The vinaigrette was generally similar to the pomander.

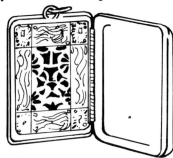

Vitrine

A small vertical eighteenth-century cabinet intended to hold curiosities and valuable objets d'art. The vitrine had a door composed of a single glass panel in order not to obscure the contents from the viewer, and usually had glass sides as well.

Voile

A soft, sheer, light fabric frequently used for curtains. It is made from various fibers.

Volute

Another name for a scroll, such as those that appear on the Ionic column capital or on the termination of some eighteenth-century furniture legs.

Vouet, Simon (1590-1649)

Early French Renaissance painter and tapestry designer. Vouet is considered one of the chief developers of Renaissance art in France.

Vries, Hans Vredeman de (1527-1606)

Sixteenth-century Dutch architect, painter, and furniture designer, who greatly influenced Dutch and English Renaissance furniture styles.

Wafer Box

A small silver container used to hold the small chips of wax used to seal letters.

Wainscot (or Panel-Back) Chair

A large Elizabethan oak armchair with an unusually tall back adorned with a crested rail and closed by panels. The chair, heavy and handsomely carved, had turned legs and stretcher bars. In some instances, the chair back was topped by a flat and carved cornice.

Waldglas

Green colored glass produced in Northern Europe during the late Middle Ages and used for common household items such as drinking cups and bowls. The greenish cast of the glass was caused by impurities in the ingredients.

Wall

The side of a house or a room. For a thorough exposition of decorative treatments of interior walls and the materials and methods to use, see *Walls and Wall Coverings,* p. 3152.

Walnut

A light brown to golden wood found throughout the world, long a favorite wood of European and American cabinetmakers for both solid and veneered furniture. Some of the finest pieces of Italian Renaissance and English Georgian furniture were made of walnut.

Wardrobe

A general term for any large vertical cabinet intended for hanging clothing. Originally, the term was applied to a small room used for storing clothing. The modern wardrobe has developed from the seventeenth- and eighteenth-century wardrobe known as an armoire.

Warming Pan

A covered shallow pan with a pierced lid, attached to a long decoratively carved pole. The warming pan was used to hold hot coals and was passed between the sheets of a bed during cold weather.

Water (or Bucket) Bench

A nineteenth-century American (Pennsylvania Dutch) kitchen cabinet constructed in two units: a lower cupboard closed by two doors and an upper stand set back from the top of the cupboard and supporting a mantel of wide shallow drawers. Simply decorated and skillfully constructed, the water bench received its name from the fact that it was used to store water and milking pails.

Watered Silk

Silk that has an unstable pattern of a wavy, shimmering, or watery appearance; also known as a moiré pattern.

Waterford

Irish glass produced in the city of Waterford during the late eighteenth and early nineteenth centuries. The Waterford glassworks produced unusually brilliant and decorative crystal.

Water Heater

A heating system for domestic hot water. Some facts about the choice of a heater and the values of water-softening apparatus are discussed in *Water Heaters and Water Softeners,* p. 3219.

Water Softener

A chemical, or chemicals, and/or the apparatus to regulate its use, for taking the hardness out of water. See *Water Heaters and Water Softeners,* p. 3219.

Watteau, Jean-Antoine (1684-1721)

Celebrated French painter influential in the development of the sinuous and complex ornamental style of the French rococo period.

Web (or Trifid) Foot

An early-eighteenth-century foot shaped to resemble three toes. The web foot was used on a cabriole leg.

Wedgwood, Josiah (1730-95)

English potter who introduced some of the finest stoneware in Europe, including the well-known jasperware. When fired, jasperware was white, but by means of metallic oxides other colors

A Wedgwood vase, decorated with designs that imitate Etruscan pieces. The red color is called *rosso antico*.

were produced, among them the familiar light blue. During the nineteenth century, jasperware was often decorated with classic figures in relief, usually white against a colored background.

Weisweiler, Adam

Late-eighteenth-century French cabinetmaker who worked in the Louis XVI style but was also considered instrumental in the formulation of the French Directoire and Empire styles. Weisweiler is noted for his delicate furniture designs.

Welting

A length of fabric, usually tubular in shape, used to reinforce and disguise seams on upholstery, slipcovers, and bedspreads.

Whatnot

An elaborately ornamented freestanding set of open shelves intended to display curiosities and objets d'art (whatnots). During the nineteenth century, the whatnot became a favorite article of furniture and it was often lavishly decorated with mirrors, carved filigree, and turned spindles supporting the shelves.

Wheel-Back Chair

An eighteenth-century chair-back design featuring a wheel with spokes of equal length radiating from a decoratively treated hub. The wheel-back chair, as with the oval-back chair, is associated with neoclassic designs.

Wicker and Rattan

Pliant twigs, canes, or osiers interwoven like basketry. They are used to make furniture and other articles. See *Wicker and Rattan,* p. 3224.

Willard, Simon (1753-1848)

American clock designer who worked in Massachusetts and is considered the inventor of the "banjo" clock, a distinctive wall clock that has a shape suggestive of the musical instrument.

William and Mary Furniture Style

Furniture and decorations associated with the reign of William and Mary (1689-1702) are so termed. During this period, Dutch, French, and other continental influences effected an emphatic transformation in the appearance of English furniture, introducing more graceful outlines and more decorative woods and hardware. This period is also referred to as early Queen Anne, since the forms that later became the fully matured Queen Anne style were introduced during this time. For more information, see *English Styles,* Vol. 7, p. 1266; and *Furniture Styles,* Vol. 9, p. 1626.

Walnut chairs in the William and Mary style. Courtesy of Metropolitan Museum of Art.

Willow Pattern

A pictorial scene, rendered in an Oriental manner, introduced on English china during the later eighteenth century. The composition presented a landscape with a pagoda, willow trees, birds, and three figures on an arched bridge.

Window

An opening in a wall to let in light and air, generally closable by one of various forms of sash or casement containing glass panes. The possible decorative treatments of windows are discussed in *Windows and Window Treatments* on p. 3228 and continued in Vol. 18.